C000269648

INTERIORS
INSPIRATION & MATERIALS

VIVAYS PUBLISHING

CONTENTS

CONTENTS

FOREWORD

Choosing materials for an interior is a genuinely engrossing experience, but it can sometimes be a stressful one. Dreams often have to be tempered by a sense of reality. However, it is worth taking some time to select the right materials. The ideal interior is a question of the right design – synthesising functionality and aesthetics. This means the choice of materials should be determined not only by their functional characteristics but also by their aesthetics.

To help in the selection of materials, a number of professionals from the world of interior design have joined forces to produce *Interiors: Inspiration & Materials*. 2voor5, specialists in architecture, construction and interior design, were responsible for developing the concept for the book. For its realisation they relied on the professional advice of Joris Roelants and Elke Verpoten of the interior designers OOG3, who provided enormous added value through their knowledge of the field and adopted an approach that was thorough and at the same time sensitive and truly inspirational. 2voor5 and numerous other experts collaborated on this project. The resulting extensive overview aims to provide clear guidance on how to choose and use the right materials, and is a perfect tool for helping get ideas across when a builder, architect and interior designer are discussing an interior.

In this book, the term 'interior' refers to the floors and walls as well as the bathrooms, kitchens and lighting. Architects and interior designers play a key role in combining the right materials while still taking account of their technical characteristics. After all, each and every material has its own specific properties influencing how it can be processed and finished, which in turn affect the ambience of a room. Creating contrasts between cool and warm materials, or conversely looking to find a balance between the two, can help pick out features or let the materials come into their own.

The chapters on Floors, Walls, Kitchens, Bathrooms and Lighting provide objective information about specific materials, accompanied by clear illustrations. Where possible, a few key plus and minus points have been listed, and there are tips about maintenance and the various possible applications. A considerable amount of space has also been given to innovative techniques and materials, drawing on the designers' technical backgrounds to provide an up-to-date picture of the multi-faceted, constantly evolving world of interior design. *Interiors: Inspiration & Materials* will, hopefully, become a never-ending source of inspiration to those interested in interiors.

With thanks to the OOG3 design studio, www.oog3.be.

FLOORS

CEMENT-BOUND FLOORS
Cast floors

Concrete is made of cement, gravel and sand. A polished concrete floor consists of reinforced concrete – strengthened with steel wire or other netting – with a polished quartz layer. There are a range of colours to choose, but allowance should be made for the fact that colour differences are inherent in this type of floor.

A concrete floor is laid by mixing and pouring the concrete directly on the spot, without a sub-floor. As concrete can easily crack, this is best done by professionals. After the concrete has been poured, the floor is covered with quartz powder and given a smooth surface using a power float (power trowel machine). Polishing the surface further will create an even stronger and more hard-wearing top layer with a dense surface structure. It is best to give the fresh concrete a supplementary treatment to limit evaporation of the water mixed in with the concrete. This can take the form of regularly spraying the floor or of placing plastic tarpaulins directly onto the concrete surface. A curing compound – a finishing layer that is glued onto the floor to create a film – can also be applied. It is important for the floor not to be exposed to freezing temperatures while drying as this may cause shrinkage that can crack the concrete.

Concrete floors are primarily used in industrial applications, and they have their own specific advantages and disadvantages. Concrete floors are non-flammable and heat resistant, and they can be combined with underfloor heating systems. Although these seamless floors are very durable and hard-wearing, they do generally develop cracks and fissures over the course of time. It is also possible that a white lime glaze may appear on the surface. This comes from the cement and is sometimes carried up by the water as it rises to the surface. However, this whitish bloom gradually disappears as a result of wear and tear. Contact with moisture can also cause rust stains. Concrete floors produce dust too, although this can be avoided by scrubbing the floor regularly. Another disadvantage is that wet, polished concrete floors are slippery. The continuous surface of a concrete floor is easy to maintain – all that is required is dry or wet cleaning on a regular basis. Even so, some materials (such as mineral greases, oils or acids) may cause indelible stains.

The price and quality of concrete floors depends on the thickness of the concrete, the reinforcement, whether quartz is added or not and the number of polishing steps.

Plus points
- ⊕ wide range of colours
- ⊕ seamless
- ⊕ very hard-wearing
- ⊕ durable
- ⊕ non-flammable
- ⊕ suitable for underfloor heating
- ⊕ low maintenance

Minus points
- ⊖ must be laid by professionals
- ⊖ susceptible to cracking
- ⊖ may produce dust
- ⊖ white blooms of lime may appear
- ⊖ rust stains are possible
- ⊖ can be slippery when wet, so not very suitable for wet areas
- ⊖ can stain

1 | 2
3 | 4

1. This seamless floor is perfectly suited to larger rooms. 2. Despite the industrial nature of the floor, the interior can still seem warm. 3. Give this type of floor enough expansion joints to avoid cracking. 4. These cement floors run through from one room to the next, making them appear larger.

1. These seamless floors are rather industrial in nature. 2. A proper protective layer allows this type of floor to be laid in bathrooms too. 3. The floor is frost-resistant and can be laid outside as well. The floor in this interior runs from inside to outdoors.

LIME MORTAR FLOORS
Cast floors

Lime mortars based on a mixture of reused lime and brick-dust were once a popular choice for less well-off people who could not afford marble or wood. These beige-coloured floors later waned in popularity and were out of fashion for quite some time. In fact, it was not until a number of mortar floors had to be restored in Italy that people became interested in rediscovering the traditional techniques used in the past. These techniques were then picked up and improved upon by floor specialists, generating renewed interest in this type of flooring. There are two variants. In the first variant, mortar floors produced according to the classical system are laid on a totally natural, hand-made sub-floor of lime and brick rubble. An appropriate limestone-based finishing layer covers the floor, followed by an oil layer. Waxing will give the floor an additional wear layer. This is a very labour-intensive, expensive method that will take about a month. However, there is another faster, less complicated process using a mixture of natural hydraulic lime, expanded silicones of various granule sizes, and water. This mixture remains usable for two hours and must be laid over a normal cement sub-floor. It must then dry for forty-eight hours and can be finished using silicate paint after two to three weeks.

These two variants give completely different results. The first method results in a genuine lime mortar floor, which often has a grainy structure and a matt look. It is not self-levelling and often still needs to be sanded. Floors that are laid using the second method have much straighter lines. They are similar to cast or poured floors, but they still look as if they were made by a craftsman.

A lime mortar floor can be combined perfectly with underfloor heating and is totally moisture-resistant. The lime base can, therefore, also be used for finishing walls, bathtubs, sinks and kitchen worktops. As only lime and brick debris are used (or indeed reused), lime mortar floors are thus very environmentally friendly.

In principle, lime mortar floors are highly resistant to stains but care needs to be taken with wine as the tannins can affect the lime. This type of floor requires very little maintenance; all that is needed is scrubbing or mopping, depending on the required effect. Lime mortar floors are fairly hard-wearing, but not hugely so. On the other hand, minor damage can always be repaired.

Plus points
➕ moisture-resistant
➕ resistant to stains (except for wine stains)
➕ environmentally friendly
➕ very low maintenance

Minus points
➖ fairly hard-wearing (but not very)
➖ can be expensive, depending on installation

1. Even though lime floors use old techniques, they fit in beautifully in modern homes. 2. A lime floor is moisture-proof and, therefore, suitable for wet rooms. 3. These floors cannot take the high point stresses of cement-bound cast floors or polyurethane floors.

1 | 2   *1. The natural appearance of this floor combines well with other natural materials such as plain wood. 2. Do not expect a perfect, mechanically smooth finish – this is done by hand.*

EPOXY FLOORS
Cast floors

An epoxy floor is a seamless cast floor made entirely of plastic, namely an epoxy resin. Like polyurethane (see page 27), this is an artificial resin, a synthetic material with the same properties as a natural resin: it can be poured, is soft and adheres well. Synthetic resin cast floors come in transparent and opaque variants. This allows creative flooring specialists to experiment with incorporating all kinds of objects in the cast floor. Some examples are slices of Parma ham, crushed fake watches, stainless steel. Experiments with added pigments are also possible, creating nebulous shapes or patterns of aluminium or gold.

As 80% of the three days required for laying a cast epoxy floor is taken up with preparing the floor, it is best to have this type of floor laid by a professional. The sub-floor is roughened and then finished with an adhesive layer to reduce the risk of craters, pits and air bubbles (which must be avoided at all costs as they may fill with dirt). A matt, satin or gloss finish is applied to the floor on the third day. The finishing is important as this determines how vulnerable the floor is to scratches. It is possible to walk on the floor after twenty-four hours, but it should not be used until after four to seven days.

An epoxy floor, like any seamless floor, can run through several rooms, which makes skirting and sills unnecessary. A cast epoxy floor is very hard-wearing, warm and soft thanks to a wear layer approximately 3 mm (approx. 0.1 in) thick. Combining the floor with underfloor heating is no problem at all. However, it is not very UV-resistant and will have to be treated with a special paint layer to prevent discoloration. A cast epoxy floor is less hard and elastic than a cast polyurethane floor and will, therefore, crack more easily if the sub-floor expands or shrinks. It is also less resistant to high point loads caused by sharp objects. Like parquet floors (see page 63), this type of floor needs to be treated with a great deal of care. The floor must be cleaned regularly with a damp mop and requires thorough cleaning once a year to remove tracks. Regular application of a new protective layer is also recommended. This type of flooring is normally watertight.

Cast epoxy floors are much cheaper than polyurethane floors. Epoxy is, in fact, a collective name for various types of plastic, so the quality and price can vary a great deal. The price will also depend on the design.

Plus points

- ➕ wide range of colours and patterns
- ➕ can be made to fit the room
- ➕ seamless
- ➕ hard-wearing
- ➕ suitable for underfloor heating
- ➕ fairly low maintenance
- ➕ usually cheaper than cast polyurethane floors (depending on the design)

Minus points

- ➖ must be laid by professionals
- ➖ not very resistant to scratches unless there is a hard top coat
- ➖ cracks easily
- ➖ UV can cause discoloration

1

2 | 3

1. This material has innumerable colour options. 2. Mixing different colours gives very different results – everything from rustic to modern. 3. This material can be used to simulate other types of floors, such as a cement-bound floor.

1. Epoxy floors can take high point loads and can be used anywhere in an interior. 2. This type of floor is also extremely suitable for wet rooms.

PEBBLES IN SYNTHETIC RESIN
Cast floors

As explained in the information on epoxy floors (see page 19), it is possible to incorporate objects in a transparent synthetic resin floor. Pebbles can also be embedded in such cast floors without any problems. Epoxy is the usual synthetic resin used in private homes. This material allows for play not only with the colours of the stones, but also with the colour of the resin. A highly natural effect is created, for example, when beige stones and colourless resin are used, or an artificial effect when using white stones and pink or blue resin. Pebbles in synthetic resin are also versatile in terms of the applications they can be used for. The technique is suitable for flooring, but can also be used as decorative cladding for walls, furniture or doors. In addition, the material is translucent, making it possible to place lighting behind walls or doors.

It is best to call in a professional to lay a floor like this. The operation will take about a week. First, the sub-floor is prepared, if necessary. The stones are then put into position, after which the resin is poured over them. Special custom-made sheets are occasionally used to cover the floor. It is polished the following day and is safe to walk on straight away.

This type of floor is very strong, durable and hygienic. In addition, using a resin gives the floor softer acoustics because the resin dampens noise. A cast resin floor can easily be combined with underfloor heating. It is suitable for intensively used rooms because it is so tough and resistant to wear and tear. The floor is laid with no joins, so it can run through several rooms without any skirting or sills being required. The floor may develop cracks in some cases as a result of the sub-floor shrinking or expanding. This type of floor is easy to keep clean as the resin has been processed to prevent stains. All that is needed is to hoover or sweep the floor regularly. After a period of time it may be necessary to polish the floor again, which effectively gives the floor an entirely new top layer.

A floor consisting of stones in synthetic resin is expensive not only because of the materials used but also because the installation always needs to be carried out by professionals.

Plus points
- ⊕ seamless
- ⊕ durable
- ⊕ hygienic
- ⊕ wide range of colours
- ⊕ resistant to stains
- ⊕ low maintenance

Minus points
- ⊖ must be laid by professionals
- ⊖ expensive
- ⊖ cracks may develop
- ⊖ difficult to make neat finishes in corners

1. Resins are transparent making it possible to put a light source under a resin floor. 2. This is the effect that is achieved when a resin floor is sanded with a diamond disc after it has cured. 3. Synthetic resin has been used here for the seating and the open hearth. The possibilities are endless!

1. Resin floors are massively strong, non-wearing and suitable for intense use. 2. These four photos show just a few of the possibilities of this versatile material. 3. Riverbed pebbles give the floor a three-dimensional effect.

POLYURETHANE FLOORS
Cast floors

Like epoxy, polyurethane is a kind of synthetic resin, or more specifically a collective name for a group of synthetic materials that always consist of both hard and soft components. This makes polyurethane not only hard but also elastic. This type of cast floor is available in about seventy colours and offers unlimited possibilities in terms of design, colour and composition. Depending on what is required, either a matt or a satin gloss finishing layer can be chosen, while coloured flakes or chips can be mixed in to give the floor a playful effect. As this type of floor is poured with no seams, it is perfectly possible to let it run through several rooms. This creates a more spacious impression and removes the need for skirting and sills. The liquid mixture can be poured onto almost any sub-floor as long as it is flat, dry and sturdy and will retain its shape. The floor has to be laid by a professional. The process generally takes about four days, with one layer being applied each day. The floor can be walked on on the fifth day, and can be used fully from day six onwards. Grit-coating by adding a layer of fire-dried quartz on the floor after it has been laid will create a non-slip coat that also protects against stains and dirt and makes the floor more hard-wearing.

Polyurethane floors can easily take high point loads. They are far more elastic and much harder than epoxy floors, so there is less risk of them cracking if the sub-floor shifts. The elasticity also makes this type of cast floor very suitable for underfloor heating. A polyurethane floor is highly resistant to UV radiation.

The floor is impermeable and dust-free making it very hygienic. It is totally watertight, resistant to chemicals and very easy to maintain. Mopping the floor once a week will suffice. Oil stains or chemical stains can easily be removed with the right products. A new layer may need to be applied after five to ten years to remove irregularities, damage and scratches. One major disadvantage of cast polyurethane floors is their strong initial odour.

Because polyurethane is a collective name for a range of different plastics, the price and quality of polyurethane floors depends a great deal on the exact material used. In general, a cast polyurethane floor is far more expensive than other synthetic resin floors and is mainly used in industrial applications.

Plus points
- ✚ hygienic
- ✚ seamless
- ✚ moisture-resistant
- ✚ permanently elastic
- ✚ very hard-wearing
- ✚ resistant to UV radiation
- ✚ suitable for underfloor heating

Minus points
- ➖ must be laid by professionals
- ➖ slippery when wet
- ➖ could be damaged by sharp objects
- ➖ expensive
- ➖ unpleasant odour when first laid

1. Cast polyurethane floors can be made in every conceivable RAL (NCS) colour. 2. This material is even suitable for garages, although a wet floor can become slippery. 3. The material needs very little maintenance and can, therefore, even be used in minimalist white.

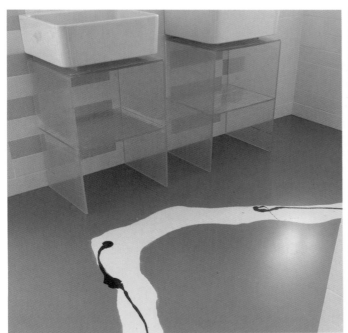

1. Different colours can be used, but they cannot be mixed together as they can for resin floors. 2. This cast floor has a warm feeling, making it ideal for bedrooms and bathrooms. 3. The flattest finishes can definitely be obtained with cast polyurethane floors.

TERRAZZO FLOORING
Cast floors

Terrazzo flooring, also known as stone carpet, quartz carpet, gravel flooring and various other names, is a seamless floor finish made of natural stone granules and a transparent artificial resin. The granules, which are 2 to 4 mm in size (approx. ¹⁄₁₀ in), are first washed, dried and graded by size. The best quality granules come from southern Germany: these are extremely hard and very clean. Colour, granular structure and finishing are fine-tuned to suit personal tastes and usage requirements. There is an almost unlimited range, with thousands of options for colours, patterns and combinations.

Terrazzo flooring can be applied to any solid sub-floor as long as it is dry, clean, flat and free of grease. The sub-floor may be tiled or even made of wood, provided it is watertight and retains its shape. The floor is cast by professionals, who pre-treat the sub-floor and then apply the granules in a layer 6 to 8mm thick (approx. ¼ in), depending on the type of granule. The floor can be walked on twenty-four hours after it has been laid and may be used fully after forty-eight hours.

Terrazzo flooring quickly adapts to the ambient temperature because of its open, grainy structure. As a result, it can easily be combined with underfloor heating. Furthermore, dust particles remain trapped between the holes in the floor rather than wafting through the room, which makes this type of floor highly suitable for people with dust allergies. A disadvantage of this open structure is that water can permeate the floor, so if a terrazzo floor is being used in areas with water, such as a bathroom or kitchen, the open structure should be filled with a transparent filler. Even then, this type of floor is fairly hard and rough underfoot if walking barefoot.

The floor is hard-wearing, fireproof and easy to clean – all that is needed is to hoover or sweep it regularly. It is a good idea to scrub the floor by machine or manually using a cleaning agent once or twice a year. If doing this, it is very important to remove the cleaning water with a water vacuum cleaner afterwards so that it cannot permeate the floor. A new coating restoring the original wear layer can be applied after ten to twenty years, depending on how heavily the floor has been used. This is not a major operation.

Terrazzo flooring is cheaper than natural stone or parquet but more expensive than ceramic tiles.

Plus points
- ✚ wide range of colours and patterns
- ✚ seamless
- ✚ non-allergenic
- ✚ very hard-wearing
- ✚ non-flammable
- ✚ suitable for underfloor heating

Minus points
- ➖ must be laid by professionals
- ➖ not resistant to moisture
- ➖ not suitable for walking on barefoot

1. Gravel flooring is very strong and can take high point loads, but it is not particularly resistant to water. 2. The material is anti-allergenic and, therefore, ideal for bedrooms. 3. This type of floor can also be used in bathrooms, as long as a proper coating is applied to waterproof it.

1. Quartz carpets are very hard-wearing and scratch-resistant. 2. The photos at the top right show how different motifs and colours can be used. Terrazzo flooring gives ample scope for creativity. 3. A gravel carpet fits in with a modern, minimalist interior or a more classical style.

WOVEN VINYL
Soft floors

This woven plastic floor covering consists of 90% vinyl and 10% polyester. The combination of plastic plus a weaving technique makes it very tough. A wide range of colours is available, and it is also possible to have all kinds of shapes, which in turn can be combined using batches of different colours because the rolls can be cut easily without fraying. Woven vinyl is also available as tiles.

It is very important to make sure that the sub-floor is flat, completely dry, not too warm and not too dirty (no oil, paint, asphalt and so forth) as otherwise this may cause discolorations or distortions. The best thing to do is to cut the floor strips and then let them acclimatise unrolled in the room for twenty-four hours. The strips are placed next to each other with a 4 cm (1 ½ in) overlap along the edges. A single cut through both pieces at once gives a neat fit with edges that are then cold welded together to give a virtually invisible, watertight seam. Woven vinyl is best laid by a professional, although skilled DIY people will be able to lay it themselves. Tiles are easier to lay than rolls.

Woven vinyl is very hard-wearing and has a long life. It is fire-proof, absorbs noise well and the structure of the fabric means that it is non-slip. However, a disadvantage is that the rigid structure of the fabric makes it seem less warm and welcoming, and it is not really suitable for walking on barefoot. It is, therefore, not recommended for playrooms, bathrooms or bedrooms. It is also unsuitable for humid areas. Woven vinyl cannot be combined either with underfloor heating.

The woven structure of these floors makes maintenance extremely easy. Because the floor is watertight, dust cannot get underneath the fabric structure and can, therefore, be removed simply by hoovering. The floor can also be cleaned with a little water from time to time while persistent stains can be treated with bleach. When cleaning, the scrubbing action should go parallel to the grain of the fabric structure. Using acetone, alkalis, abrasives or strong solvents is not recommended as they can cause damage.

Finally, woven vinyl is very affordable.

Plus points	Minus points
⊕ durable	⊖ rough, rigid surface
⊕ non-flammable	⊖ not suitable for walking on barefoot
⊕ noise-dampening	
⊕ non-slip	⊖ not suitable for underfloor heating
⊕ non-allergenic	
⊕ low maintenance	⊖ not suitable for humid areas

1. Woven vinyl is available in tiles or as full-width rolls. 2. Cold-welding the material allows a seamless floor to cover a large space.

1 | 3

2

1. The woven plastic has a fine structure, but it is very tough. It can be used both indoors and out. 2. This floor covering has the same luxurious look as fitted carpet, and the advantages of a synthetic floor. 3. Vinyl collections are updated every year to reflect the prevailing trends.

CARPETS
Soft floors

Carpeting can either be fitted (also known as 'broadloom' carpets) or can consist of loose rugs or carpets, which may or may not have special edging. Fitted carpets are being used less and less often in family homes now for reasons of hygiene, but rugs are still frequently used to cover existing floors. Carpets are available in all kinds of shapes, dimensions, colours, patterns and textures. The length, nature and thickness of the pile determine not only the look of the carpet but also how it feels. Carpets are woven by hand from natural or synthetic fibres, or tufted, woven, flocked or knitted by machine. The pile can then be sheared or cut in a range of different ways, giving a different result each time. The pile length may also vary a great deal, with high and low (or long and short) pile carpets, for example. The quality and lifespan of a carpet depends on its composition, pile structure and how it was manufactured. A hand-knotted or hand-tufted woollen carpet tends to be more durable than a synthetic tufted carpet. Sufficient information should be obtained from the supplier before buying any particular type of carpet.

Carpets reduce noise, are soft and pleasant to walk on and feel slightly springy or resilient. The material is naturally textured, making it almost impossible to slip on. Fitted carpets combined with underfelt are not really suitable for rooms with underfloor heating. Using carpets in kitchens and bathrooms is also not recommended as they only have limited resistance to moisture and stains. The biggest disadvantage of carpeting, though, is that it can harbour dust mites. The excreta of these small creatures may cause allergies if they stick onto dust particles that are then inhaled.

Synthetic carpets can be hoovered vigorously immediately after being laid but wool carpets initially require somewhat more caution: only short and gentle movements should be used at first. Periodic cleaning will keep a carpet in optimum condition.

The price of a carpet depends to a large extent on the type of fibre and how the carpet was manufactured. A hand-knotted Persian wool rug is obviously much more expensive than a synthetic carpet made by machine.

Plus points
- ✚ wide range of colours, designs, sizes and structures
- ✚ warm and comfortable
- ✚ springy
- ✚ noise-dampening
- ✚ relatively low maintenance

Minus points
- ➖ can be affected by moisture
- ➖ can stain
- ➖ allergenic

1	2
3	4

1. Carpets give any interior a warm feeling. 2. When picking a rug or carpet, thought should be given to how it will be used. Light colours and pure wool, for instance, are more vulnerable when used intensely. 3. Woollen carpets can now also be obtained in full-width rolls. 4. Fitted carpets need to be fixed to the floor.

1. Long-pile carpets are generally used in living rooms or places where people walk about less. 2. It is impossible to give a full overview of all carpet types, but this example shows how creative designers can be! 3. The quality and lifespan of a carpet depend on how it is put together. Information about construction and durability should be obtained from the sales staff, and an indiciation given of where the carpet is to be laid.

LEATHER RUGS AND MATS
Soft floors

Leather wall and floor covering is made of naturally tanned, painted cattle hide, processed under pressure with a wax solution. Leather floor covering comes in two types: mats or rugs, and tiles. Leather rugs are available in various designs. The leather can be put onto a carpet backing, which gives the rug a more rigid structure. A second type of leather mat is a patchwork of braided leather strips, which are not placed on a backing and are, therefore, thinner and more vulnerable. Tiles are only available in a limited number of colours and with smooth or antiqued finishing.

It is best to let leather tiles acclimatise for a week or two in the room where they are to be installed, kept out of direct sunlight. The tiles can simply be glued onto the floor, which should be flat, dry and dust-free. There are also magnetic tiles, which can be used on any underlying floor after first laying a metal sheet. Leather feels comfortable, is hard-wearing and resilient, and has a pleasant odour. In addition, this material is naturally a good absorber of sound and it is fire-retardant.

Dust cannot penetrate leather; it just stays on top, which is a plus point for people with dust allergies. In addition, the imprints of furniture feet will disappear very quickly. Although the material is water-repellent, which prevents moisture from permeating, leather tiles or rugs are still not recommended for humid areas, such as bathrooms or kitchens. Rugs with a carpet backing cannot be combined with underfloor heating, but floor coverings made of multiple pieces of leather can. Leather tiles can also be used in combination with underfloor heating as long as the temperature changes are gradual.

Leather rugs and mats can be cleaned using a vacuum cleaner (with a head with soft bristles) and a damp mop. Water can easily be dabbed off, and persistent stains removed with a little water after they have dried. Aggressive products must never be used, but beeswax can be used to wax the leather floor once or twice a year.

Leather floor coverings are extremely luxurious and exclusive and are, therefore, expensive.

Plus points
+ slightly springy
+ noise-dampening
+ hard-wearing
+ fire-retardant
+ resistant to humidity
+ non-allergenic

Minus points
- expensive
- limited range of colours
- unsuitable for humid areas
- not always suitable for underfloor heating
- affected by acids

1. Woven leather has a very special aura. 2. Leather tiles are often placed on metal surfaces and attached with magnetic strips. This makes it easy to move tiles around and the floor can acquire a uniform patina. 3. Patchwork is a more affordable solution and all sorts of variants on the theme are available. 4. Patchwork rugs of animal hides are very contemporary and hard-wearing.

1. Their hard-wearing nature and stain resistance makes patchwork rugs ideal under the dining table. 2. Dyed hides are now available which can be used to produce wonderful combinations. 3. Patchwork rugs can be made easily to size. 4. Leather tiles can be used on the wall or the floor, exuding a feeling of ultimate luxury.

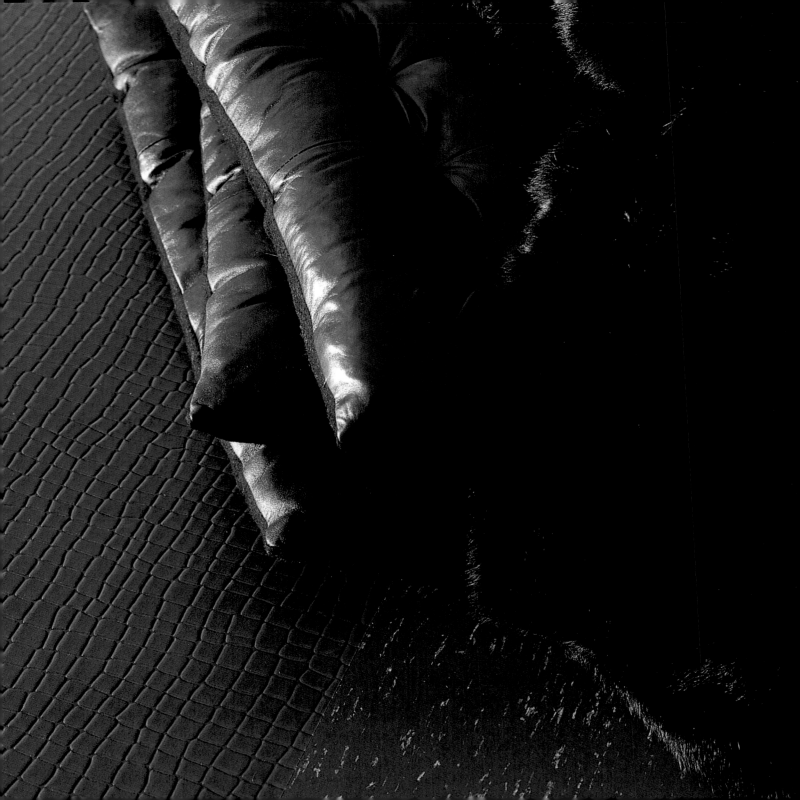

LINOLEUM FLOORS
Soft floors

Unlike vinyl (see page 51), linoleum is made entirely of natural raw materials. It is an elastic floor covering made up of linseed oil, wood dust, cork powder, resins, chalk and jute – components which are fully biodegradable. Linoleum is an excellent material for creative floor ideas as it is available in a wide range of colours, geometric patterns and finishes (for instance with patterning added in relief), and it is easy to combine colours and designs. It is also available as tiles, backed with glass fibre rather than jute so that it will not shrink.

Laying linoleum requires a professional approach. However, anyone good at DIY will have no trouble with linoleum tiles that click together. The floor beneath should always be smooth, flat, clean, sufficiently compression-resistant and permanently dry to avoid blistering.

The linoleum must acclimatise first for forty-eight hours before it can be laid. The seams are welded together, making them almost invisible. Afterwards the floor can be given an attractive shine by polishing it with a gloss coating wax. Once the floor has been laid it will have a yellow sheen, but that discoloration will disappear once it has been exposed to sunlight.

Linoleum is anti-static, which means it does not attract dust or dust mites, and is, therefore, non-allergenic. It can last twenty-five to thirty years, making it one of the most durable floor coverings. In addition, linoleum is comfortable, not too hard underfoot and reasonably non-slip. But it is definitely not water-resistant: the material will rot if water gets into the seams. On the other hand, it can be combined with underfloor heating.

The normal upkeep of linoleum involves no more than hoovering to remove loose dust particles and sand grains, which may cause scratches. The floor can be cleaned more thoroughly with a mop and a mild detergent, but care should be taken not to use too much water because of the limited moisture resistance of this flooring. Linoleum also does not take heavy-duty solvents.

This floor is by no means the cheapest floor covering available, and having it laid by a professional can also push up costs considerably.

Plus points
- ➕ wide range of colours and patterns
- ➕ highly durable
- ➕ does not need to be laid by a professional
- ➕ environmentally friendly
- ➕ anti-static and non-allergenic
- ➕ warm
- ➕ suitable for underfloor heating

Minus points
- ➖ not scratch-resistant
- ➖ rather expensive

1. Linoleum is available in rolls or as tiles. 2. Linoleum is excellent for creative floor ideas. Numerous designs are available, with or without relief patterns. 3. The seams of full-width linoleum rolls are glued together invisibly.

1 | 2
—
3

1. Linoleum is ideally suited for intensive use, such as in the office here. 2. Different patterns can be laid next to each other and glued seamlessly. 3. When the room's entire floor is covered, the effect of a cast floor is achieved.

VINYL FLOORS
Soft floors

A high-quality vinyl floor consists largely of pure PVC (polyvinyl chloride). Vinyl floors are always made up of five layers: two wear layers, a transparent or non-transparent printed design layer, a colour layer and a stippled bottom layer, made from the residue of the other layers. But vinyl is still very thin despite all these layers. The key advantage of vinyl flooring is its versatility and flexibility. Almost perfect imitations of wood or natural stone, modern print designs with a glass or metallic look, or ultra-modern visual effects like glitter patterns, are all possible. Different colours and designs can also be used in combination.

As this floor has to be laid accurately following the proper procedures, this is best done by a professional, although handy DIY people could lay the floor themselves. The usual format for vinyl is tiles, in standard thicknesses. These are glued to the underlying floor, which is always prepared in the same way and must be clean, sufficiently smooth, permanently crack-free and dry. It should also have a minimum temperature of 13°C (55°F). The vinyl and the products need to acclimatise first and to attain a temperature of at least 17°C (63°F) before the strips can be laid, cut and glued.

The quality of a vinyl floor depends on the purity of the PVC. The layered composition of vinyl makes it very durable and hard-wearing. Vinyl floors last longer than wooden floors because of vinyl's greater resistance to temperature fluctuations. They are also more resilient than ceramic tiles and will not be damaged if sharp objects fall on them. However, they do not last as long as linoleum. Vinyl is less moisture-absorbent and reflects sounds more than laminate, and it is more hygienic and less allergenic than carpet. The PVC prevents the corners from curling when moisture is absorbed, which would release unpleasant gases and odours. Vinyl is, therefore, a highly water-resistant and non-slip type of flooring, perfect for laying in humid areas, such as bathrooms and kitchens. Vinyl can also be combined with underfloor heating. Finally, it retains its colour well.

Vinyl tiles require very little upkeep. Weekly cleaning with a vacuum cleaner or a brush followed by a mop and a cleaning agent will suffice. The tiles are also resistant to most household stains. Care should be taken so that sharp-edged furniture feet do not leave tracks. Vinyl is certainly not the cheapest floor covering, but it is good value for money.

Plus points
- ✚ durable
- ✚ non-allergenic
- ✚ moisture-resistant and non-slip
- ✚ noise-dampening
- ✚ suitable for underfloor heating
- ✚ low maintenance
- ✚ good value for money

Minus points
- ➖ furniture feet can easily leave tracks/marks
- ➖ quality depends on the purity of the PVC
- ➖ negative image, but vinyl is becoming increasingly popular again

1 | 3
—
2

1. The four photos at the top left show that vinyl is available in all sorts of designs, both in rolls and as tiles. 2. Vinyl gives good value for money and is, therefore, very suitable for company premises. 3. This type of flooring is also suitable for kitchens as it is hygienic, waterproof and low-maintenance.

1. The quality of the vinyl depends strongly on the purity of the PVC. 2. A vinyl floor scratches relatively easily. 3. As it is made from pure PVC, it is the ideal floor covering for a bathroom.

CORK FLOORS
Soft floors

Cork comes from the bark of the cork oak, which is removed by hand without damaging the tree. The bark grows back afterwards, making cork a very environmentally-friendly product. After being removed the bark is ground up and the granules pressed together and baked. Most cork comes from Spain and Portugal, and cork from the Algarve in particular is renowned for its high quality. Cork naturally has a warm colour and is very comfortable underfoot because of its structure. Picking a product with a transparent protective coating allows the typical cork patterning to be retained, but numerous colours and effects are possible as well, including marble or granite. However, a cork floor exposed to bright sunlight may discolour very quickly. Cork floors may be made from tiles, parquet boards or strips, or rolls.

A cork floor can be laid by amateurs who are handy at DIY. The cork does need to acclimatise for forty-eight hours in the room where it is going to be laid. A dry, flat underlying floor is always required. The format determines how the cork floor is laid: tiles are easiest and usually have tongues and grooves that are glued together. Parquet boards or strips can also be laid using a floating or a click system. Forty-eight hours after being laid, the cork is finished with a number of layers of lacquer that protect the floor against water and dirt. Each layer of lacquer must be dry before the next one can be applied. The final lacquer layer takes twenty-four to forty-eight hours to dry, after which the floor can be walked on. Some cork floors have already been lacquered in the factory.

Cork flooring is quite springy, putting less stress on knees, joints and back than other floors. Moreover, cork is resistant to point loads and dampens noise well. It is hygienic, anti-static, non-allergenic and fairly durable. It is reasonably non-slip even when wet, which means it can also be used in bathrooms, although it is important that the floor has a layer of lacquer to protect it properly against moisture. Cork is warm and conducts heat, and consequently quickly adjusts to the ambient room temperature. However, it cannot be laid over underfloor heating systems as this lifts the tiles.

Regular sweeping, hoovering and cleaning with a moist cloth are recommended. The finish coating can be restored periodically back to its original state by first sanding the floor and then re-lacquering.

Cork floors are very affordable.

Plus points
- ✚ does not need to be laid by a professional
- ✚ slightly springy
- ✚ non-allergenic
- ✚ noise-dampening
- ✚ hard-wearing
- ✚ moisture-resistant
- ✚ very affordable

Minus points
- ➖ UV can cause discoloration
- ➖ not suitable for underfloor heating
- ➖ generally requires special finishing

1 | 3
---
2 |

1. Cork is non-slip and therefore safe for bathrooms. 2. If cork is used in the bathroom, it has to be treated with a water-resistant lacquer layer. 3. Cork floors have a pleasantly soft and warm feel.

1. The material is very springy and resilient. 2. Cork dampens noise well. 3. Cork floors cannot be used with underfloor heating.

1 | 2
  | 3

AGED WOOD FLOORS
Wooden floors

New wood can be made to look like time-worn wood in just three days thanks to a unique aging and colouring process. Newly produced planks from non-threatened European oaks are given random dents and marks with a machine, after which the wood is treated with a water-based wood dye to give subtle gradations in colour. The final result is a rustic wooden floor that is hardly distinguishable from an 'authentic' old floor. Unlike old wood, these artificially aged floors are available in a wide selection of colours, thicknesses and patterns.

This treatment method has numerous advantages when it comes to laying the floor. One is that there is no longer any need to sand the floor after it has been laid. So, although professional installation and finishing are still required, the process is less labour-intensive. The underlying surface must be dry, insulated and firm to get a good result. The floorboards are glued, nailed or laid as a floating floor, just like parquet, and the floor can be walked on after only one day.

The quality of a wooden floor depends on the type of wood chosen. Aged wood has the charm, look and feel of real old wood but the robustness and durability of new wood. The floor is hygienic, non-allergenic and warm. It gives a clean, taut impression, yet at the same time it is a little springy. However, aged wooden floors are not water-resistant and are highly sensitive to temperature fluctuations. Underfloor heating can be used in combination with an aged wooden floor under certain conditions.

An aged wood floor requires less maintenance than a normal wooden floor. Weekly cleaning with a vacuum cleaner, brush or mop will suffice. The floor must be cleaned thoroughly every one or two years. Persistent stains can be removed with a slightly moist cloth, but large amounts of water or aggressive cleaning products should not be used. Putting felt pads under furniture feet is also recommended so that they do not leave marks.

Aged wooden floors are quite expensive because of the intensive production and finishing process.

Plus points
- ✚ old parquet appearance but with all the advantages of new wood
- ✚ wide selection of colours, designs and thicknesses
- ✚ warm
- ✚ non-allergenic
- ✚ suitable for underfloor heating under certain conditions
- ✚ springy
- ✚ relatively low maintenance

Minus points
- ➖ must be laid by professionals
- ➖ not resistant to moisture
- ➖ sensitive to fluctuations in air humidity
- ➖ expensive

1 / 2 | 3

1. The odd extra scratch doesn't matter – it is part of the charm of this material. 2. These floors must not be sanded again once they have been laid. Laying them is, however, a skilled job. 3. Artificially aged floors suit all styles, both modern and traditional.

1. The floors are just as scratch-resistant as normal floorboards. 2. The five photos on the right show that aged boards can be laid in all sorts of patterns. They are available in numerous shades, but in general they are more expensive than new wood.

◀ *Solid parquet floors are available in a wide range of types and sizes. They add a luxurious cachet to the interior.*

FLOORS   63

PARQUET FLOORS
Wooden floors

Parquet consists of one (solid parquet) or several layers of wood, with an upper layer that is at least 2.5 mm thick (approx. $^1/_{10}$ in). If the upper layer is thinner than 2.5 mm, it is called veneer (see page 75). Parquet floors can be laid in various patterns, such as a herringbone pattern, a chequerboard or braided pattern, or laid next to each other like floorboards. Parquet flooring is available in various types of wood, such as oak, beech, maple, chestnut and wengé. Each wood has its own specific structure, and some may discolour under the influence of light and oxygen after they have been laid.

The various kinds of parquet can be distinguished depending on how they have been laid: mosaic parquet, with the wooden pieces glued onto panels; carpet parquet, with the wooden parts placed directly on the covering floor; tongue-and-groove parquet, with wooden parts that click together; and end grain wood parquet. Installation is best left to a professional, although a competent DIY person should be able to install floating tongue-and-groove parquet. The underlying surface must be dry, insulated and firm to get a good result. The parquet is glued, nailed or laid floating. The wood is then varnished, waxed or oiled, each of these treatments giving a different result. A polished floor has a warmer, softer colour than a varnished floor, whereas an oiled floor has a natural, untreated look. In all cases the floor can be walked on after just one day.

The quality of the floor depends in part on the type of wood used. Parquet is warm and durable. It is thermally insulating and only suitable for underfloor heating under certain conditions. Certain types of wood are affected by moisture, and an appropriate type of wood needs to be selected for rooms with considerable fluctuations in air humidity and temperature. Parquet floors are hygienic and non-allergenic. All floors must be hoovered or swept regularly, and polished parquet must be waxed occasionally. Varnished parquet can be treated with a polish a few times a year and oiled parquet must be scrubbed once a year using a special soap. The finishing layer will also need to be redone in the course of time. Small scratches are easily sanded away, but it is best to have wooden pieces with substantial damage replaced by a professional.

The price of parquet depends on the type of wood and the method used to lay it, but in general this is an expensive form of flooring.

Plus points
- ✚ wide selection of wood types, patterns and finishes
- ✚ warm
- ✚ durable
- ✚ non-allergenic
- ✚ suitable for underfloor heating under certain conditions
- ✚ low maintenance
- ✚ easy to repair

Minus points
- ➖ best laid by professionals
- ➖ affected by fluctuations in air humidity
- ➖ not always resistant to moisture
- ➖ expensive

1. To lengthen a narrow room visually, boards should be laid parallel to the longest wall. 2. The herringbone pattern is often used in older town houses. 3. Parquet is available in all sorts of sizes and colours, but can vary greatly in price.

1 | 2 / 3 *1. The horizontal slats are continued in the kitchen table to create a uniform whole. 2. Solid parquet adds value to the house. 3. Parquet can be used in all rooms of the house, but must have the right protective layer or treatment.*

BAMBOO PARQUET FLOORS
Wooden floors

Bamboo is a high-quality alternative to other wood types. In fact, bamboo is not a tree but a type of grass that lignifies and grows very fast. Whereas it generally takes fifty years before an oak is ready for timber production, bamboo is ready for production after just four to six years. The stalks then simply regrow from their roots again, so there is no shortage of bamboo plants and bamboo wood. Bamboo has a recognisable structure because of its characteristic knots. It is available as floorboards and as tiles. The colour of bamboo is restricted to white (non-treated) or caramel (after treatment with steam under pressure).

The floor can be laid without any difficulties, although calling in a professional is recommended because the installation and floor finishing are important factors in determining the quality of the floor afterwards. Professionals know best how to lay a floor to maximise the noise-dampening effect. Bamboo can be glued, nailed or laid floating, depending on the type of floor. After laying, the floor can be oiled or lacquered (varnished) to give the required result: an oiled floor has a natural look, whereas a varnished floor has a glossy look.

The characteristics of bamboo can best be compared to those of oak, but bamboo is harder, with even a minimum thickness producing a very robust result. Bamboo is also durable and hard-wearing, and can last for decades when properly maintained. It is not very porous and is, therefore, stain-resistant. This type of floor is less sensitive to fluctuations in air humidity than other types of wood and will shrink or expand less quickly. Even so, long-term exposure to extreme humidity will be harmful. A bamboo floor is compatible with underfloor heating, providing it is glued directly onto the concrete. This can best be done by a professional. If bamboo is used in a bathroom a join must be left, which is then filled with elastic silicone, and the floor should also have an additional protective coating.

Bamboo is hygienic, non-allergenic and extremely easy to maintain. Regular cleaning with a vacuum cleaner or a slightly damp cloth prevents sand grains or other dirt particles from damaging the parquet. If damage does occur, the affected area can be touched up with varnish. The parquet should be sanded down and lacquered or oiled after five to eight years.

The price of bamboo parquet is similar to the price of oak parquet, but the rolls and veneer design variants are cheaper.

Plus points

➕ very hard and tough, hard-wearing

➕ very environmentally friendly

➕ non-porous and stain-resistant

➕ hygienic, non-allergenic

➕ not so sensitive to fluctuations in air humidity

➕ suitable for underfloor heating under certain conditions

➕ low maintenance

Minus points

➖ limited range of colours

➖ is best laid by professionals

➖ not resistant to moisture

1. Bamboo floors are easy to lay. 2. Inlaid work is one of the many possibilities of bamboo parquet. 3. This type of wood is also very suitable for bedrooms.

1
2 3

1. Bamboo is a very hard-wearing wood that can take high point loads and is hardly porous. 2. Bamboo is very suitable for rooms where people walk around a lot. 3. Despite its versatility, bamboo is available in fewer colours than other types of wood.

◄ End grain wood is the toughest and longest-lasting wooden floor.

FLOORS   71

END GRAIN WOODEN FLOORING
Wooden floors

End grain wooden flooring is the toughest parquet floor currently available. Its strength is due not to the type of wood but to the way the wood is processed. This type of parquet floor consists of numerous small, generally square wooden blocks sawn across the wood grain (whereas traditional parquet wood is sawn along the grain). This gives an end-on view of the annual growth rings. The wood types generally used for end grain parquet are gua-tambu (sometimes known as ivory wood), hornbeam, kambala and merbau.

Laying this floor is labour-intensive and requires craftsmanship. It is very important that the sub-floor is dry; the underlying floor should also not be moist and should be strong enough to absorb pressure. The blocks are glued directly onto it and pressed by hand up against the previous row, which will create enough space for the blocks to settle. It is also possible to use prefabricated panels in which the blocks are already combined on a net. The floor must not be laid in very dry conditions or under high temperatures. After the parquet floor has been laid it is sanded until it is even and then treated with oil, varnish or wax. Each treatment gives a different result: a waxed floor has a warmer and softer tint than a varnished floor, whereas an oiled floor has a natural, untreated look. The floor can be walked on after just one day.

Because of its structure, end grain wood has much better resistance to loads. This parquet is relatively hard-wearing and, therefore, ideal for intensive use. End grain wood is also particularly effective in sound proofing as the vibrations are absorbed along the wood fibres more quickly than in other types of parquet. This kind of floor is warm, hygienic and non-allergenic. However, the open pores of end grain wood make it very sensitive to fluctuations in air humidity, and it is definitely not resistant to moisture. It is, therefore, unsuitable for use in areas where water is used, such as in kitchens and bathrooms. End grain wooden flooring can be used in combination with underfloor heating. The amount of maintenance this type of floor needs depends a lot on the finishing. All floors must be hoovered or swept regularly. Waxed parquet must be polished now and then, while varnished parquet can be treated with a polish a few times a year and oiled parquet must be scrubbed with a special soap. Furthermore, the life of a parquet floor can be extended by periodically carrying out restoration of its finishing layer. Individual pieces of end grain wood can be replaced easily. End grain wood is not very common and is more expensive than normal parquet.

Plus points
- ➕ warm
- ➕ very hard
- ➕ durable
- ➕ extremely hard-wearing
- ➕ non-allergenic
- ➕ noise-dampening

Minus points
- ➖ must be laid by professionals
- ➖ not resistant to moisture
- ➖ affected by fluctuations in air humidity
- ➖ hard to sand because of its extreme hardness
- ➖ very expensive

1 | 2 / 3   *1. Parquet in end grain wood is extremely durable and well-suited to intensive use. 2. Because of its durability, end grain wood is often used in public spaces. 3. This material has to be laid by professionals, which is a labour-intensive process.*

1. Because it is so hard, end grain wood is seen as the precursor to tiling. 2. It is however sensitive to fluctuations in humidity and temperature. 3. The blocks are sawn perpendicularly across the long axis, so the annual growth rings in the wood are visible.

VENEER PARQUET FLOORS
Click systems

Veneer is an extremely thin layer of high-quality wood applied to a very hard, water-resistant HDF (high density fibreboard) sheet. There are also wood veneer floors with cork backing, which have the same springiness and noise-dampening characteristics as cork. Veneer is distinct from multi-layer parquet in that the top wooden layer is thinner than 2.5 mm (approx. $1/10$ in). Laminate is different again: a paper photo print is applied as the top layer rather than high-quality wood (see page 79). Several different types of wood are used for the production of veneer wooden floors, including oak, beech, cherry, birch and wengé. All retain their unique grain structure, giving a uniform yet versatile floor. Moreover, different veneers can be combined with each other. It is also possible to give the wood V-grooves, which emphasise the floorboard effect.

Veneer parquet can be laid over any dry existing floor and the wood is available in tongue-and-groove planks that click together easily. It is perfectly possible for a non-professional to lay the floor, although it is important to remember to allow for the wood's patterning. This loose-laid floor can be walked on immediately after it has been laid.

Veneer parquet is an environmentally-friendly alternative to solid parquet as it requires far fewer trees for the same floor area. The material is strong and hard-wearing but will not last as long as solid parquet, where the upper layer can be repeatedly sanded and refinished as necessary. The different varnish layers applied during the production process make the flooring scratch-resistant, elastic and highly resistant to damage. It is also anti-static and non-allergenic. It is virtually impossible for dirt to accumulate because of the smooth surface structure. Veneer parquet is also warm and can be combined with underfloor heating. Although the boards are treated with paraffin to offer additional protection against penetrating water, they are still unsuitable for humid areas, such as bathrooms and kitchens. Maintenance is best done without liquid, but a damp cloth, with an appropriate maintenance product in dilution, can be used. Excess water should be avoided. Stains can best be removed with methanol or denatured alcohol. Veneer is much cheaper than normal parquet.

Plus points

⊕ warm, with high-quality wood used for the top layer
⊕ hard-wearing
⊕ environmentally friendly
⊕ suitable for underfloor heating
⊕ low maintenance
⊕ cheaper than solid parquet
⊕ non-allergenic

Minus points

⊖ less durable than solid parquet
⊖ dampens noise less well than solid wood
⊖ unsuitable for humid areas

1. A thin layer of real wood is glued onto an HDF board, which sometimes has a tongue-and-groove system. 2. Laminated parquet is more suitable for underfloor heating than solid parquet. 3. It is also possible to give the wood V-grooves that emphasise the floorboard effect.

1. Veneer is a more affordable way of using rarer wood types such as walnut. 2. Laminated parquet can have a cork backing that improves the springiness and dampens noise. 3. Like solid wood, veneer can be used in any room as long as it is treated properly first. The thinner wood layer (2.5 mm / $^1/_{10}$ in) does make it less durable.

LAMINATE FLOORS
Click systems

Laminate is an environmentally-friendly alternative to wooden floors as it does not consume natural resources. It is based on HDF sheeting, which is made of fine wood fibres that have been compressed to a high density and glued to make them watertight. The more the fibres are compressed, the better the quality. A pattern layer (a photo print) is placed on top and a transparent melamine coating on top of that. Under the HDF sheet is a backing layer, which protects against moisture and ensures stability. Laminate is available in an extensive assortment of patterns and colours, ranging from wood to stone and textile prints. Moreover, laminate can now be provided with V-grooves and relief patterns, which means that these floors can barely be distinguished from solid wooden floors. Laminate boards or tiles can easily be laid over existing floors. They should be left in their packaging and allowed to acclimatise for forty-eight hours in the area where the floor is to be installed. The floor underneath must be dry, smooth and dust-free. The click system allows floors to be laid very easily without the need for glue. The boards should be laid in such a way that incidental light entering the room shines lengthwise along them.

The floor can be used as soon as it has been laid. The durable upper layer ensures a strong, colour-fast and very scratch-resistant floor. The floor is also resistant to most types of stains and is hygienic. The closed surface structure makes it impossible for dust and other dirt to adhere to it, which means these floors are non-allergenic.

Laminate can also be combined perfectly with underfloor heating. However, laminate floors should not be installed in humid areas, such as bathrooms and kitchens, because although the top coating is water-resistant, the core is not. Laminate used to be considered noisy, both for the room itself and for other rooms below, but nowadays noise-proof underfloors are used to solve this problem.

Laminate floors require very little maintenance. Unlike wood, laminate must not be sanded or waxed. A regular hoover and a good clean with a damp mop and some hot water will suffice. If there are persistent stains, these can best be removed with acetone, white spirit or turpentine. Small damaged areas can be filled in; larger ones will require the affected board to be replaced.

Laminate is much cheaper than a solid wooden floor.

Plus points
- ➕ nowadays looks increasingly like real wood (with the V-groove)
- ➕ non-allergenic
- ➕ durable
- ➕ scratch-resistant
- ➕ resistant to stains
- ➕ suitable for underfloor heating
- ➕ very low maintenance

Minus points
- ➖ cheap image
- ➖ artificial
- ➖ not suitable for humid areas

1. Laminate is not wood. The top layer, designed to look like wood, has a more artificial appearance. 2. Laminate is a good choice for a living room because it is more resistant to scratches than a solid parquet floor. 3. Moisture-resistant laminates have recently been developed. They have black rubber joins between the boards.

1. Better quality laminate floors now also have V-grooves cut in that make them look even more like real wood. 2. Because it is relatively cheap, laminate is often used in bedrooms. 3. Laminate floors are an affordable and versatile alternative for any room.

CONCRETE TILE FLOORS
Hard floors

Concrete is the simplest flooring material and is made up of cement, gravel and sand. A concrete floor can be mixed and poured on the spot (see Cement-bound floors, page 11) or laid as tiles or sheets.

As concrete can crack, laying this type of floor is a job for professionals. Concrete tiles are cast in advance and then laid on location. The floor can then be finished in various ways. It can be polished or ground, painted using special paint, or waxed. The concrete can also be coloured using gypsum pigments, which create a soft, matt look. Repeated layers of artificial resin can give the floor a glossy reflection. If the concrete is mixed with special gravel, and then milled and polished after it has hardened, a granite-like effect is achieved.

New kinds of concrete floors are continually being created. B-tone concrete tiles are made from refined concrete, reinforced with quartz and coloured with a minimum amount of colour pigment. These tiles are very hard-wearing. They are available in two formats (50 x 50 cm and 50 x 80 cm, 19 ¾ x 19 ¾ in and 19 ¾ x 31 ½ in), in two thicknesses, in two shades of grey and with a brushed or smooth finish. Concrete floors must be given a protective coating to avoid dust formation. Because of the versatile character of concrete floors, they can be used in all areas of a home, both indoors and out. Smooth, polished concrete surfaces can, however, be slippery when they are wet, but this problem can be solved by treating the floor with artificial resin or by adding pebbles while casting.

Because concrete tiles are cast beforehand, there will be no scale or rust formation, as is the case with a cast concrete floor. Tile floors are porous, so oil, mineral greases and acids may leave marks. Irrespective of the floor finishing, concrete is always extremely easy to maintain. A tepid solution of water and soap will suffice. Concrete tiles are also suitable for underfloor heating and they are heat-resistant and non-flammable.

Plus points
- ➕ very hard-wearing
- ➕ durable
- ➕ low maintenance
- ➕ heat-resistant
- ➕ non-flammable
- ➕ suitable for underfloor heating

Minus points
- ➖ must be laid by professionals
- ➖ slippery when wet
- ➖ liable to crack or break while being laid
- ➖ can stain
- ➖ affected by acids

1 | | 3
2 |

1. *Concrete tiles are good for humid environments. 2. As concrete tiles can be slippery when wet, care is needed. 3. Concrete tiles can be placed on the walls as well as the floor.*

1. When these tiles are polished, they can look grainy and smooth. 2. Tiles like these take craftsmanship: every tile will look slightly different.

CERAMIC TILE FLOORS
Hard floors

Ceramic tiles are made from fine, ground clay that is compressed into shape under high pressure and then baked at high temperatures. Industrial ceramic tiles have regular dimensions and colours. There is an extensive range of colours, designs, shapes and sizes. The size varies from 1 x 1 cm (approx. ½ x ½ in) for mosaic tiles to 60 x 120 cm (23 ½ x 47 in) for large tiles. It is also possible to incorporate other materials such as rubber, glass, aluminium or stainless steel into them. Most tile makes have small variations in size, but these differences are compensated for at the joins. Nowadays tiles can also be sawn to precise sizes after the baking process. As a result, these rectified tiles are always exactly the same size, which will limit the size of the joins (approx. 2 mm, 1/10 in). Furthermore, grouting in the same colour as the tiles is available and many tile collections have matching skirting boards and inner and outer corners.

Ceramic tiles are laid in cement or glued to the underlying floor with tile adhesive. These tiles should be laid by a professional. If they are to be glued, the ground should be completely dry, smooth and hardened. The floor can be walked on after three days and loads placed on the floor after seven days. The tiles have to be laid in cement if they vary in thickness or if the underlying floor is not entirely smooth. The underlying floor still needs to be dry and hardened if this method is used. The tiled floor can be walked on after five days, but full loads have to wait for twenty-eight days. The substantial improvement in the quality of tile adhesive over recent years means many professionals now prefer gluing the tiles to using cement.

The tiles are hard, durable, non-flammable, strong and hygienic. Fully glazed tiles are also resistant to frost. They are always cool but are nevertheless suitable for underfloor heating. Because of their hard structure they reflect sound and are not springy underfoot. Wet ceramic tiles are usually very slippery, but there is an extensive range of slip-proof tiles for bathrooms.

Ceramic tiles are watertight and resistant to marks and are, therefore, low maintenance. The floor needs to be mopped with hot water and a cleaning agent, followed by mopping with clean water. If necessary, persistent stains made by acidic liquids can be removed with turpentine.

Price and quality may vary considerably because of the extensive range of ceramic tiles available. More information about the new generation of ceramic tiles can be found on page 213.

Plus points
- ● wide range of colours, sizes, designs and structures
- ● hard-wearing
- ● durable
- ● resistant to stains
- ● humidity-resistant
- ● suitable for underfloor heating
- ● very low maintenance

Minus points
- ● must be laid by professionals
- ● cool
- ● noisy
- ● no springiness

1 | 3
—————
2 |

1. An industrial product with a craftsman-like look. 2. Ceramics take point stresses well and are hard-wearing. 3. Rectified tiles hardly need grouting any more.

1. The latest generation of tiles are available in sizes up to 100 x 300 cm (approx. 3 x 10 ft). 2. Because they are so thin, they can be laid on top of an existing tile floor.

3. Ceramics are the ideal materials for wet areas.

MOSAIC FLOORS
Hard floors

Mosaic is pure floor and wall art. It consists of small blocks or pieces of hard material, such as marble, stone, coloured glass, stainless steel, terracotta or ceramics, that are combined together and glued in place. The floor has a luxurious look because the various pieces all catch the light in their own way. Glass mosaic comes in various designs (matt, mother-of-pearl and translucent) and in more than a hundred colours. About forty different types of marble mosaic are available. The numerous possibilities in terms of materials, colours, patterns and designs allow mosaics to be used very imaginatively. It is not only possible to concoct colourful patterns using the small tiles, larger surfaces can also be created using the same colour – a technique that can be integrated in a modern interior. Moreover, single-coloured tiles are available in different sizes and patterns. Mosaic sections can also be incorporated in floors made from other materials, like wood and concrete.

Mosaic can be laid on floors of any size. Installing a mosaic floor requires know-how and craftsmanship. It used to be a very complex and labour-intensive process, but nowadays much of the material is prefabricated. Although the patterns are still made by hand, they can be arranged beforehand and glued onto nets, which in turn can be cut into variable shapes. They are then laid on the spot as just a few large, composite pieces. Floors with blocks of all the same colour are entirely mass-produced.

It is important to have the right information about the best grouting to use for the joins between the tiles. Too much moisture can result in mould that is often very hard to get rid of. Using a two-component filler (grout) can avoid a lot of serious problems.

Mosaics have the same characteristics in terms of moisture resistance, temperature sensitivity, abrasion resistance and so on as the material they are made of. The difference in structure between mosaic and attachment creates a slip-proof relief, which makes the material highly suitable for bathrooms and shower rooms.

The maintenance of the floor also depends on the material used. Marble mosaics must be cleaned in the same way as natural stone; glass mosaics only require soap and water. Mosaic floors are usually expensive.

Plus points
- ➕ wide range of colours
- ➕ wide range of materials
- ➕ non-slip
- ➕ exclusive
- ➕ the same plus points as the material the mosaic is made of

Minus points
- ➖ must be laid by professionals
- ➖ expensive
- ➖ the same minus points as the material the mosaic is made of

1. Any mosaic has its own technical specifications and is, therefore, not suitable for all purposes. 2. This replica of a Persian rug is a warm element in the bathroom interior.
3. Because laying a mosaic floor is manual work, all sorts of motifs can be built in.

1. Glass mosaic tiles give options for original lighting. 2. If a motif is repeated several times, templates can be used.

◀ *Using steel for flooring is highly original and certainly worth considering. Even so, it is rarely used in private homes.*

FLOORS   95

STAINLESS STEEL
Hard floors

Stainless steel studded floors consist of thin sheets with studs pressed into them. The floor is only available in a single colour – steel grey. The studs give grip on what would otherwise be a slippery steel floor, and also allow functional and decorative patterns to be created. The standard dimensions of the sheets are 120 cm x 60 cm (47 x 23 ½ in), but they can be laser cut according to requirements. The flooring can be painted or have stickers attached without any problem. The steel sheets can also easily be combined with other materials, such as wood or natural stone.

The floor sheets are glued onto the concrete underlying floor with a special glue. First, an adhesive layer is applied to the dry, dust-free substrate layer and to the steel sheets, after which the floor is lubricated with glue. The sheets are then placed 1.5 mm (¹/₁₀ in) from each other. Finally, the joints are filled with the same glue. The floor can be walked on after one day at most. Because steel sheets are conductive, they need an anti-static coating and must be properly earthed to reduce the risk of electrocution.

Contrary to what might be expected, a stainless steel floor is not noisy at all. In fact, the adhesive layer between the concrete and the floor sheets absorbs noise, provided that this layer has been applied properly. The material is durable, hard-wearing and scratch-resistant. Although stainless steel has a cool look and feel, it is still a floor that is well able to absorb and retain the heat of the underlying concrete. However, this type of floor cannot be combined with underfloor heating.

Stainless steel flooring is extremely hygienic and low maintenance. Hoovering or mopping is sufficient as this floor does not absorb dust. Small surface scratches can easily be removed by polishing the floor. The best way to restore the steel floor's completely new, shiny look, removing all tracks and marks, is to clean it once every five years using a scrubbing machine and a fine abrasive.

This type of floor is rather expensive because of its labour-intensive installation.

Plus points

✚ can be cut to fit the room
✚ highly durable
✚ hard-wearing
✚ conducts heat
✚ anti-static coating
✚ non-allergenic
✚ very low maintenance

Minus points

➖ only available in one colour
➖ labour-intensive installation
➖ cool
➖ exclusive, therefore difficult to find someone able to install it
➖ rather expensive
➖ not suitable for underfloor heating

1. & 2. These industrial steel grilles let light through in a surprising way.

1. These studded sheets are mostly used on company premises and are very pricey. 2. A steel mezzanine gives a handsome industrial look, but can be very noisy. 3. A steel floor in a kitchen can get slippery.

BASALT
Natural stone

Basalt is a volcanic igneous rock formed by the solidification of lava. Because it cools very rapidly, its minerals do not have much time to crystallise, which gives the stone its fine-grained look. Basalt is characterised by light colour nuances on a dark-grey background.

Natural stone floors are best laid by professionals. A traditionally laid floor installed on a dry underlying floor can usually be walked on after five days. The floor can be used after about a month, but needs at least three months to dry completely. The use of water must be restricted to a minimum while the floor is drying, and it is best cleaned during this period by hoovering. If the floor has been glued onto a dry underlying floor it can be walked on after just three days, and will be ready for use after seven days. It takes another month before it is totally dry.

This stone type can be used in its raw form, but can also be processed. While polishing the floor will emphasise the colours and create a high shine, polished basalt floors are sensitive to scratches and very slippery. Indeed, polishing natural stone floors is not recommended as this wears the stones down more quickly. Basalt can also be 'honed', a process in which the floor is sprinkled with water and sanded until it is semi-matt. This will make the tiles slightly reflective and smooth, and no grooves will be visible. Like polishing, honing also makes the stone more sensitive to scratches.

Basalt can be combined with underfloor heating, although specific conditions then need to be observed. In general, natural stone easily absorbs heat and conducts it gradually. It is also acid-resistant, hard-wearing and very tough. This type of stone is also well suited for use as terrace tiles.

Basalt is hardly porous at all and, therefore, only needs a special impregnation agent to be applied after the floor has been laid in order to protect it against dirt and stains. Such an impregnation agent will not change the appearance or character of the stone.

It is a good idea to use floor mats as well. Regular cleaning with a vacuum cleaner or a slightly moist cloth prevents sand grains or other dirt particles from damaging the floor.

Like any natural stone, basalt is expensive. This is not only because of the installation, but also due to the high transportation and processing costs.

Plus points
- very tough and hard-wearing
- acid-resistant
- not very porous
- suitable for underfloor heating

Minus points
- must be laid by professionals
- polished or honed basalt floors are not scratch-resistant
- polished floors can be slippery
- expensive

1. There are few colour nuances in this stone, giving the floor a homogenous appearance. 2. Basalt is not a very porous rock, making it ideal for kitchens and dining rooms.

1. Honed basalt has a darker colour. 2. When basalt is polished, it becomes smoother and more liable to get scratched. 3. Basalt is available in all sorts of shapes and sizes, and this type of stone can create a restful and harmonious whole.

BLUESTONE
Natural stone

Bluestone is a dark, compact type of limestone that may contain fossil remnants, such as petrified molluscs and plants. Colours range from light grey to dark blue-grey depending on the finish. Belgian bluestone is particularly popular, although the Asian variant is increasingly being used as well. Both have a similar origin, composition and properties. However, Chinese bluestone contains a lot of dolomite, which may give it a brown glaze after a while.

Natural stone floors are best laid by professionals. A traditionally laid floor installed on a dry underlying floor can usually be walked on after five days, and can be used after less than a month. The floor needs at least three months to dry fully, during which time it should be hovered regularly and as little water as possible used. A glued floor with a dry underlying floor can be walked on after just three days, and will be ready for use after seven days, although it takes another month before it is totally dry.

A characteristic property of bluestone is its hardness. Despite this it can still be processed. Polishing the floor will emphasise the colours and create a high shine, but this also makes the floor susceptible to scratches and very slippery. Indeed, polishing natural stone floors is not recommended as it wears the stones down more quickly. The stone can also be honed, with the surface being sprinkled with water and then sanded. This will make the tiles slightly reflective and smooth, and no grooves will be visible. This process also makes the floor susceptible to scratches. Slight waves and saw cuts can be created by sawing the stone with a frame saw, diamond wire or a diamond cutting disc.

Bluestone naturally absorbs heat and conducts it gradually, which makes the stone ideal for use with underfloor heating. Bluestone is durable, hard, hard-wearing and slightly porous and, therefore, highly suitable for use outside. Any scratches that do occur tend to be visible, but the more veins the stone has the less the scratches stand out. This kind of floor is quite sensitive to acids, especially if it has not been honed, but it can be treated to withstand acids by using an impregnation agent or a water-repellent product.

The floor should be maintained by applying linseed oil soap with a little water. This should not be rinsed but can be dried afterwards using a tepid, squeezed-out mop. The soap will nourish the floor and fade small scratches. To make the floor to shine again, it can be polished with wax and a machine.

Plus points

⊕ hard-wearing
⊕ durable
⊕ suitable for underfloor heating
⊕ frost-resistant
⊕ low maintenance

Minus points

⊖ must be laid by professionals
⊖ polished and honed floors are not scratch-resistant
⊖ polished floors can be slippery
⊖ rather porous
⊖ affected by acids

1. The presence of fossils makes bluestone very distinctive. 2. This material is extremely scratch-resistant, which makes it good for intensively used areas like hallways.

3. A floor of small rough tiles that runs through to the outside enhances the spaces.

1. This type of stone works well in both rustic and modern interiors. 2. The group of photos on the right shows how versatile bluestone can be in the home, but it is still natural stone and can stain.

◀ *Sandstone generally conjures up an image of pale-coloured stone. However, it is available in many colours, including some very dark ones.*

FLOORS   107

SANDSTONE
Natural stone

Sandstone is a porous sedimentary rock made from compacted sand and usually has a warmer look than igneous rock, such as granite or basalt. The most common colours of sandstone are white, cream, yellow and red. The appearance of the stone can be regular or irregular. The use of sandstone is not recommended as fine quartz dust, which may cause the lung disease silicosis, is given off during the processing of the stone.

Natural stone floors are best laid by professionals. A traditionally laid floor installed on a dry underlying surface can usually be walked on after five days. The floor can be used after about a month, but needs at least three months to dry fully. The use of water must be restricted to a minimum while the floor is drying, and it is best cleaned during this period by hoovering. A glued floor with a dry underlying surface can be walked on after just three days, and will be ready for use after seven days, although it takes another month before the floor is totally dry.

Sandstone usually has a matt finish but some types of sandstone may be honed. These are sprinkled with water while being sanded ('wet sanded'), which gives a semi-matt, smooth finish. Sandstone is less suitable for polishing because it is not very hard-wearing.

A sandstone floor is frost-resistant and can be laid outside as well. Impregnation of the floor is important as the porous structure of sandstone makes it sensitive to stains. The impregnation agent does not change the appearance of the stone. Although not very hard-wearing, sandstone is more hard-wearing than limestone. Moreover, it can be combined with underfloor heating without any problems. Polished sandstone is more resistant to water and more scratch-resistant than non-processed sandstone. On the other hand, any scratches that do occur show up less on non-processed floors than on polished floors.

Upkeep of this type of floor consists of regular cleaning with a vacuum cleaner or a slightly moist cloth. This will prevent sand grains and other dirt from damaging the stone.

Plus points
- ✚ more hard-wearing than limestone
- ✚ suitable for underfloor heating
- ✚ frost-resistant
- ✚ low maintenance

Minus points
- ➖ quartz dust, which can cause silicosis, is produced when sandstone is processed
- ➖ must be laid by professionals
- ➖ less suitable for polishing
- ➖ porous
- ➖ can stain
- ➖ affected by acids

1 | 3
2 |

1. Because sandstone is porous, it is important to lay it properly. 2. Unprocessed versions show scratches less quickly than polished designs. 3. Polished sandstone is more resistant to water than unprocessed sandstone.

1. These samples give a clear idea of the different kinds of sandstone. 2. Sandstone can be laid in the same patterns as parquet. 3. Sandstone may be a somewhat less hard-wearing stone, but a little wear and tear can give that typical, aged appearance. 4.The bigger the tiles, the more calming the effect. In this example, the tiles are 60 x 60 cm (24 x 24 in).

SLATE
Natural stone

Slate is a sedimentary rock consisting of petrified clay layers. There are a lot of different types of slate, each type depending on the sort of clay that it was made from. Colours range from dark green to dark brown, dark grey and black. Some types have a metallic sheen because they contain shiny glass-like minerals. Slate is strongly layered and the natural split surface of this rock gives it a rather rough appearance, although some types of slate can be relatively smooth. Slate is often used as roofing, but it can be used inside the house as well.

Natural stone floors are best laid by professionals. A traditionally laid floor installed on a dry underlying surface can usually be walked on after five days. The floor can be used after about a month, but needs at least three months to dry fully. The use of water must be restricted to a minimum while the floor is drying, and it is best cleaned during this period by hoovering. A glued floor with a dry underlying surface can be walked on after just three days, and will be ready for use after seven days, although it takes another month before the floor is totally dry.

Slate usually comes unprocessed, but it can also be honed where the stone is sprinkled with water and sanded. The resulting surface is smooth, semi-matt and without visible grooves. Slate is fairly watertight and hardly porous. Flaking may occur sometimes because of the stone's predominantly layered structure, but this will scarcely be noticeable due to the rough surface. If necessary, flaking can be avoided by impregnating the stone. The impregnation agent does not change the appearance of the stone at all. Some slate types can be used for outdoor flooring, but not all types of slate are frost-resistant. Slate can be combined perfectly with underfloor heating as the stone conducts heat well. Slate stone is not resistant to acid. Slate flooring is easy to maintain using a well wrung-out mop and a special product, if necessary.

This type of stone is less expensive than granite or marble.

Plus points

⊕ not very porous
⊕ suitable for underfloor heating
⊕ low maintenance
⊕ cheaper than granite or marble
⊕ fairly moisture-resistant

Minus points

⊖ must be laid by professionals
⊖ not always frost-resistant
⊖ affected by acids
⊖ flakes can chip off

1. Beautiful results can be obtained with slate. 2. The three photos, bottom left: slate is available in various forms and can also be used in kitchens. 3. Every tile is unique.

1. Unsmoothed slate has numerous colour nuances and an attractive range of shades. 2. Natural stone is the ideal flooring for in front of an open hearth. 3. When slate is laid in an irregular pattern, the effect is less restful.

MARBLE
Natural stone

Marble occurs when limestone metamorphoses at very high pressures and temperatures. The fossils that can be found in limestone are no longer recognisable in the marble. Marble is light in colour, often with darker veins, natural colour nuances and a crystalline structure. The veins that can be found in marble are the result of impurities in the limestone. One of the best known types of marble is carrara, from the Italian city of the same name.

Natural stone floors are best laid by professionals. A traditionally laid floor installed on a dry underlying surface can usually be walked on after five days, and can be used after less than a month. The floor needs at least three months to dry fully, during which time it should be hovered regularly and as little water as possible used. A glued floor with a dry underlying surface can be walked on after just three days and will be ready for use after seven days, although it takes another month before the floor is totally dry.

Marble is easy to process. It can be polished, with the surface being sanded until it shines and the colours become stronger. However, this finish is not recommended for marble floors as this type of rock is not really hard-wearing. Marble can also be honed and the stone sanded until it is semi-matt and smooth. Other finishes, such as granulation or flaming, which tone down the colour, will not have much effect as marble already has a light colour.

Marble is softer, less hard-wearing and less tough than granite. It is also porous and not resistant to acid. If used in the kitchen, marble will definitely need a protective layer. Impregnation protects the floor against dirt and stains, and reduces permeation of liquids and chemicals. Impregnation agents do not affect the appearance of this stone. Marble is water-resistant and can also be combined with underfloor heating without any problems. Most types of marble are frost-resistant and can, therefore, be used outside as well as inside. Marble floors can best be cleaned using hot water and nourished with a special product. However, the use of the wrong maintenance products may cause stains or dull marks.

This natural stone is rather expensive, although there are cheaper variants, in the form of tiles, on the market today.

Plus points

⊕ suitable for underfloor heating
⊕ usually frost-resistant
⊕ moisture-resistant
⊕ luxurious appearance

Minus points

⊖ must be laid by professionals
⊖ less hard-wearing than granite
⊖ porous
⊖ affected by acids
⊖ expensive, but there are cheaper variants in the form of standard tiles
⊖ additional protection is required if it is to be used as kitchen flooring

1
---
2 | 3

1. Polished marble is less porous and the surface will be shiny. 2. Natural stone can be cut into all sorts of shapes and sizes. 3. Marble is a hard stone and hard-wearing. It is very good for stairs.

1. Marble is very popular with interior designers again. 2. These samples give an idea of the various types of marble. 3. Marble is equally at home in a rustic or modern interior.

LIMESTONE
Natural stone

Limestone is a sedimentary rock composed of calcite deposits, for example from marine organisms, which are then petrified. This relatively soft stone usually has a warmer look than igneous rock, such as granite or basalt. Limestone has a highly variable surface structure with veins, marks, splashes and sometimes even clear traces of fossils. It is available in both light and dark colours, ranging from cream and yellow through red and brown to grey and black.

Natural stone floors are best laid by professionals. A traditionally laid floor installed on a dry underlying surface can usually be walked on after five days and used after about a month, although it needs at least three months to dry fully. Use of water must be kept to a minimum while it is drying; it is best cleaned during this period by hoovering. A glued floor on a dry underlying floor can be walked on after just three days and is ready to use after seven. It takes another month to dry fully.

The limestone surface can be processed in all kinds of ways, resulting in a shiny, matt or rough look. Polishing is not a very suitable treatment for limestone because this stone is not particularly hard-wearing. Honing is possible though and this involves the stone being wet sanded while sprinkled with water, which makes it semi-matt and smooth. This process will, however, affect the colour of the limestone.

The properties of limestone are generally similar to those of marble. It is a less rigid and more porous type of stone, which makes the floor susceptible to stains. Impregnation is, therefore, recommended, particularly if the stone is used in a kitchen or bathroom. Limestone is rather soft and consequently liable to scratching. Limestone floors are suitable for underfloor heating. A few kinds of limestone flooring are frost-resistant. A limestone floor can best be cleaned with a mop, using a special product if required. Stains can be removed with a liquid cleaning agent or a gel.

Plus points

- ⊕ wide range of colours
- ⊕ suitable for underfloor heating
- ⊕ very warm look and feel
- ⊕ some types are moisture-resistant

Minus points

- ⊖ must be laid by professionals
- ⊖ less suitable for polishing
- ⊖ less hard-wearing
- ⊖ porous
- ⊖ can stain
- ⊖ not scratch-resistant
- ⊖ affected by acids

1 | 3
2

1. Limestone can be obtained in both rough and polished forms. 2. There can be large colour variations within a single batch. 3. Limestone provides a warm element in a modern interior.

1. Polished limestone does not stain easily and can be used in kitchens. 2. The samples above show that limestone can have very different surface structures. 3. Limestone can be used either in rustic styles or in minimalist interiors.

PEBBLES IN MORTAR
Natural stone

Pebbles cast in mortar create a very natural effect. Designs can be played with endlessly: creating patterns and recurring themes, combining different colours, etc. There is virtually no end to the range of pebbles available – and, consequently, considerable variation in shapes – some pebbles are flat, others are angular. Pebbles can be used to create a smooth surface, but their volume can also be emphasised by letting them stick out. There are ready-made designs on sale, with pebbles mounted on a net-like surface. There are also techniques for setting pebbles in wood, which creates a striking effect, with the warm, soft look of the wood contrasting with the rather hard and cool pebble components. Mortared pebbles are not only used as flooring but also as wall covering.

Installation should be done by a professional. The underlying floor must be properly prepared, with all the irregularities removed, and must be thoroughly dry to ensure proper adhesion of the glue. Loose pebbles can be laid in cement, but this method is not recommended as it is very labour-intensive and has to be done accurately, otherwise the pebbles could come loose. A better option is to use the pebbles that are pre-glued in nets. These are laid on the underlying floor, after which the spaces between the pebbles are filled with mortar. Proper information should be obtained about the right product if grouting is to be added between the pebbles. The recommendation is often to use grouting of the same colour as the pebbles. Filling the gaps with mortar should be done carefully as the pebbles must not be covered and no mortar residue must remain. The randomly applied pebbles are sometimes not very random at the edges of the sheets, so it is possible that the separating line between two strips will remain visible. This effect can be partly eliminated by using smaller pebbles. There are also products available that give the pebbles increased shine, making them stand out more.

Cast floors containing pebbles are hard-wearing, durable and moisture-resistant, making them very suitable for areas where water is used, such as kitchens and bathrooms. These floors are, however, fairly expensive.

Plus points
- ✚ wide range of colours, designs and shapes
- ✚ hard-wearing
- ✚ durable
- ✚ moisture-resistant if laid correctly

Minus points
- ➖ underlying floor must be prepared properly
- ➖ must be laid by a professional
- ➖ has to be laid accurately
- ➖ expensive

1 | 2
  | 3

1. This material adds a natural touch to a bathroom. 2. If the pebble surfaces are polished, it makes the upkeep of the floor easier. 3. River pebbles also massage the soles of the feet.

1. Pebbles can also be used in a shower, although the relief structure will make soap residues and dirt more awkward to remove. 2. River pebbles can be used on walls as well as floors. 3. The four photos bottom right: pebbles in cement become a real eye-catcher when used in moderation.

WALLS

PAPER
Wallpaper

Paper wallpaper is still widely used. One of the reasons for this is because it is one of the cheaper materials available and, therefore, an excellent choice for decorating one wall in a different colour or with a different pattern. A wide range of creative options is available – from matt to gloss and even metallic colours (see page 145). The structure of the paper may also vary a great deal. There is even paper wallpaper that looks like textile, with artificial fibres applied electrostatically to create a velvet effect. Borders are also obtainable, which allow features to be picked out and wallpapers with different colours and patterns to be combined; the border being pasted over the seam.

Paper wallpaper is available in rolls and can be hung fairly easily. The surface must first be made completely smooth: paper wallpaper is usually thin, which means any irregularities will easily show through. The wallpaper paste should be applied evenly. Pre-pasted wallpaper is also available, which only needs wetting. Paper should not be cut too short – a margin of 5 cm (2 in) needs to be left. When using a pattern, allowance should be made for the fact that some paper will be wasted because of the need to ensure the pattern on the various pieces matches up. A special roller can be used to make sure the joins fit properly. The best way to cut away edges round doors or sockets is to use a knife and a syringe can be used to apply extra paste. Minor errors can be repaired easily. For example, blisters can be pricked with a fine needle and excess paste or air pushed out of them.

Paper wallpaper often used to contain wood and did not keep its colour well if exposed to sunlight, but nowadays most such wallpaper is wood-free. Sensitivity to moisture remains a problem, so that aspect needs to be taken into account. Some types of paper wallpaper are rather thin, which means they tend to be non-washable and can tear easily. Of all the different types of wallpaper, paper will last longest as it allows the wall to breathe, which means there will be much less blistering and so on.

Paper wallpaper can be removed easily by soaking it off or by using a steam stripping machine.

Plus points

- ⊕ fairly cheap
- ⊕ wide selection of colours, designs and structures
- ⊕ quality is better than it used to be
- ⊕ usually resistant to UV
- ⊕ easy to apply
- ⊕ easy to remove

Minus points

- ⊖ rather thin
- ⊖ non-washable
- ⊖ can be affected by moisture
- ⊖ may blister
- ⊖ can tear
- ⊖ surface must be smooth

1 | 3
2 |

1. Horizontal stripes make the wall look longer and lower. 2. Wallpapers are available in all sorts of colours and motifs. 3. Wallpaper can emphasise an interior style.

1. The colours of the wallpaper can be matched to the furniture. 2. Nature is an enormous source of inspiration for wallpaper designs. 3. Wallpaper is available in an innumerable range of patterns.

VINYL
Wallpaper

Vinyl is a plastic, in this case applied to an underlayer of cotton, paper or non-woven fabric so that it can be hung easily. Vinyl wallpaper, which is heavier than paper, comes in various thicknesses or even as vinyl foam, which has a rather elastic feel. Vinyl wallpaper is available in a wide range of colours and creative designs, with relief patterning or even a silk-like texture, so there are many different things which can be done with it. Vinyl can also be painted over, but it is important to get information about the right type of paint to use.

Vinyl wallpaper can be hung by non-professionals, although special wallpaper paste is needed. Because the material is thicker than paper, the strips have to fit together well at the join: a thick, easily visible seam will be created if they overlap. If necessary, any overlapping wallpaper can be cut away to create a new seam.

Vinyl is durable and lasts a long time. Unlike paper, however, vinyl does not allow the wall to breathe and this may cause blisters over the course of time. Because vinyl is a more heavy-duty product than paper, it is good for covering up irregularities in the wall and it is tear-resistant. It is moisture-resistant as well, so it can be used in kitchens and bathrooms. Vinyl is also washable, making it ideal for children's rooms and playrooms. Because vinyl is applied with a special wallpaper paste, it is more difficult to remove than fleece wallpaper (see page 137). Moreover, the upper layer is waterproof. The best way to remove it is to make cuts in the top layer or remove it entirely, then to soak the bottom layer with a wallpaper remover or steam wallpaper stripper and strip it off.

Plus points

- ⊕ camouflages irregularities
- ⊕ durable
- ⊕ humidity-resistant
- ⊕ washable
- ⊕ rather heavy
- ⊕ does not tear

Minus points

- ⊖ is best hung by professionals
- ⊖ artificial look
- ⊖ more difficult to remove than non-woven fabric wall coverings
- ⊖ non-porous

1
—
2 | 3

1. Vinyl wall coverings are heavier than paper. 2. Using ton-sur-ton colours gives this dining room a simple unity, despite the powerful pattern of the wallpaper. 3. Vinyl wallpaper can have a relief pattern.

1 | 2

3

1. This type of wallpaper lasts a long time. 2. Care should be taken with damp walls as this type of wallpaper does not breathe. 3. Vinyl wall coverings last longer than normal wallpaper.

FLEECE
Wallpaper

Non-woven fabric wall covering, also known as fleece wallpaper, is made from various fibres, such as polyester, viscose or even cellulose, compressed into a single layer together with a number of binding agents. There are two main advantages to fleece: new aesthetic possibilities – as the structure is more fibrous than paper – and the decorative elements that can be included in the structure, like flax or petals. Fleece wallpaper is also easy to hang.

It is important the surface is prepared very carefully before hanging. The wall should be smoothed first and then insulated with a primer – thin non-woven fabrics can be transparent. Good quality fleece wallpaper is made mainly of polyester fibres. It is a synthetic material that does not absorb water, so the fibres do not swell up. Consequently, unlike with paper, the paste does not need to be absorbed by the wallpaper; it can simply be applied to the wall and the dry fleece stuck onto it. A wallpaper table is then no longer needed. As fleece keeps its size and shape, there will be no blisters or open seams. Paper should not be cut too short – a margin of 5 cm (2 in) needs to be left.

If using patterned wallpaper, allowance should be made for the fact that some paper will be wasted because of the need to ensure the pattern on the various pieces matches up. A special roller can be used to make sure that the joins fit properly. The best way to cut away edges round doors or sockets is to use a knife.

Good quality, heavy fleece wallpaper deals with cracks in plastered walls without any difficulty. Moreover, fleece wallpaper is impact-resistant and almost impossible to tear. It can be painted over, printed on or a coating applied to it to create various effects, like a glossy surface. Fleece is biodegradable and, therefore, environmentally friendly. It lets water vapour through, preventing the walls from moulding.

Light fleece wallpaper can be removed easily, but a stripper will be needed for heavier types.

Plus points
- ➕ wide range of structures
- ➕ paintable
- ➕ easy to remove
- ➕ keeps its shape and size well
- ➕ environmentally friendly
- ➕ resists moulds and moisture
- ➕ does not tear and can take a knock

Minus points
- ➖ surface must be prepared before hanging
- ➖ thin layers are transparent

1 | 3
2 |

1. Fleece wallpaper is environmentally friendly. 2. This material is strong and all sorts of decorative elements can be applied to it. 3. A wallpapering table is not needed for this material: the paste can be applied straight onto the wall.

1. Fleece keeps its shape: there are no blisters or gaps between seams. 2. It is a porous wall covering, so mould cannot develop. 3. Simplicity can look great.

TEXTILE
Wallpaper

Textile wallpaper is made from natural or synthetic fibres, such as silk, cotton, linen, jute or wool, that are attached to an underlying paper or non-woven fabric layer. It is possible to incorporate patterns in the wallpaper. A common method for doing this is flocking, where the fibres that make the pattern are applied to the textile using heat and pressure. Logos are often printed in the same way.

Textile wallpaper creates a special, warm atmosphere. The colours are often selected to enhance this effect, which explains why warm red colours are found so frequently in collections. An unusual impression is created with taffeta, a rich, glossy silk or viscose fabric that feels delicate to the touch and is very densely woven. It has a characteristic double-weave finish that makes the fabric seem alive and also changes its colour depending on the angle it is viewed from and where the light is coming from. Sunlight, artificial light, morning and evening light will all alter the appearance of the wallpaper.

There is no single standard method for hanging textile wallpaper as the procedure depends on the underlying material (non-woven fabric or paper). Paste is applied to the wall if the underlying layer is of non-woven fabric, but to the wallpaper if it is paper-based. Although fleece wallpaper is very light and flexible, non-professionals are still advised to obtain plenty of information about the proper method for hanging or to call in a professional.

Textile wallpaper can attract dust as it absorbs polluting dust particles from the air indoors that may then be released again later. This process can be curbed by treating the wallpaper with a dust-repellent and water-repellent agent. Even so, people who are sensitive to dust might be better off choosing another type of wallpaper. Textile wallpaper can also be treated with a water-repellent agent. Because the wallpaper consists of two layers, it will not tear easily.

This type of wallpaper can be stripped using a steam wallpaper stripper machine or a chemical remover. The appropriate method depends on the type of paste used.
Textile wallpaper is rather expensive, but of sound quality.

Plus points
- ⊕ warm look
- ⊕ special effects
- ⊕ does not tear

Minus points
- ⊖ allergenic
- ⊖ rather expensive
- ⊖ is best hung by professionals

1 | 2 / 3   *1. Textile wall coverings are relatively pricey, but very luxurious. 2. Even silk can be used for wall coverings. 3. Textile wall coverings create unusual effects.*

1. The subtle structures in textile wallpapers give the wall a 'warm' appearance. 2. Special weaving techniques bring the material to life – and candlelight gives yet another effect.

METAL FOIL
Wallpaper

How can you make a proper wall covering out of aluminium foil? That was what the inspired designer David Winfield Wilson asked in 1955. He was looking for techniques for printing onto aluminium foil, which was used for packaging food items, and it was only a number of years later that he got the desired result. Even so, it was hardly an obvious choice to use this extremely thin aluminium as wallpaper.

The basis of metal foil wallpaper is thin aluminium foil made of 99.5% pure aluminium. The metal is melted and made into thick sheets that are rolled into increasingly finer layers. Foil wallpaper used to have a paper backing but nowadays the layers are applied to a non-woven material. This material looks like textile, except that it is not made of knitted or woven yarn or thread. Instead, carded polyester fibres are unravelled, laid parallel to one another and bonded. A fleece is made from this material and used as the base for the metal foil.

The assortment of shades and patterns has expanded considerably over recent years. Fixed oxidation is used for some types, while others have printed patterns. Foil wallpaper conjures up an image of precious metals, giving a stylish, luxurious appearance. The use of a non-woven material base makes hanging this wallpaper much easier, but it still requires some expertise and it is, therefore, better to ask a professional for advice. The surface must be dry, clean and absorbent. All irregularities should be removed beforehand to make sure the surface is entirely smooth. This wallpaper contains conductive material and should not be used in wet areas, such as bathrooms or kitchens. Metal foil wallpaper is very robust and does not tear easily. It also stands up well to sunlight.

This type of wallpaper is, however, more expensive than paper wallpaper.

Plus points

⊕ wide range of shades of colour and designs

⊕ not affected by sunlight

⊕ does not tear

Minus points

⊖ not suitable for humid areas

⊖ more expensive than conventional wallpaper

⊖ must be hung by professionals

1 | 3
2 |

1. *This material is totally UV-resistant. 2. It can also add a luxurious touch to any room. 3. Metal foil wallpaper does not tear easily.*

1. This type of wallpaper is also impressive in a stately hallway. 2. Metal foil wallpaper should not be used in wet rooms, because metal is conductive. 3. Professionals should hang this material as it is too expensive to waste.

RELIEF
Wallpaper

Entire walls can be given a striking three-dimensional pattern using relief wallpaper, or alternatively by incorporating panelling, friezes or other items that look like ornamental plastering. This type of wall covering is made exclusively from natural raw materials: a mixture of wood pulp, wax and linseed oil. There are not only classic patterns but also new designs that can be used creatively in a modern interior. Structures such as rolled-up ropes, sea grass and sugar canes are guaranteed to appeal to the imagination. There are also narrow or broad borders for panels, ceilings and friezes to experiment with, while corner profiles make sure that edges match up perfectly.

This wallpaper is available in rolls, and detailed hanging instructions come with the product. To achieve a proper end result, the surface must be dry, firm, degreased and as smooth as possible. If the wall has cracks, a smooth glass fibre paper should be applied to cover these in the plasterwork. If there are no cracks in the wall it is still worth applying a layer of smooth fleece wallpaper to improve adhesion. A special paste is used to hang relief wallpaper. The wallpaper needs to dry for at least twenty-four hours and can then be finished in various ways; decorative techniques, such as painting, marbling, patinating (see page 173) and varnishing, create a very luxurious end result.

Relief wallpaper retains its shape and is firm, durable and impact-resistant. There is very little chance of tears or cracks because the underlying surface consists of glass fibre wallpaper or fleece wallpaper. On the other hand, relief wallpaper may accumulate more dust than a smooth wall covering.

If relief wallpaper is used for panelling, friezes and other ornamental features, it works out cheaper than standard plasterwork as it saves substantially on the hours of labour involved.

Plus points
- ⊕ luxurious look and feel
- ⊕ durable
- ⊕ natural
- ⊕ retains its shape

Minus points
- ⊖ is best hung by professionals
- ⊖ surface must be smooth, dry, fixed and clean
- ⊖ can accumulate dust

1. This technique has been in use for over one hundred years. 2. Relief wallpaper is now being used increasingly in contemporary interiors, although it still has a vintage look.

1. Relief wallpaper lasts a long time and can be painted over repeatedly. 2. This kind of wallpaper is also often used on ceilings. 3. It can also be used for edging walls.

WALLPAPER FROM DIGITAL PHOTOGRAPHY
Wallpaper

People who want to add a personal touch to their interior can use digital photography to produce wallpaper with a picture or design printed on it. Fleece is almost always the material used for this as it is stronger than paper.

Various ready-made designs are available, but a favourite picture or design can be printed onto the wallpaper. This could be an image covering the entire wall, a detail or a collage of pictures. Almost anything is possible – a poem, a work of art, a red rose, the surface of water or images reminiscent of 1970s poster wallpaper.

The first step is to get the picture printed on the wallpaper. Then the underlying surface needs to be prepared. It should be as smooth as possible to obtain a better final image and must preferably be clean, dry and have an even colour. If the image has a light basic colour, care must be taken that the underlying wall surface does not show through. Use a primer as sub-layer. There are various different methods for hanging digitally printed wallpaper. It can be glued to the wall; the fleece does not need to absorb the paste first as it does not expand. It is also possible and very easy to put the paste directly on the wall. There is even the option of pre-pasted digital wallpaper, which does not require extra paste. Digital wallpaper can also be supplied in the form of a poster. If very large, the poster will be delivered in several pieces with codes showing clearly how everything fits together. A spirit level should always be used to ensure the pieces are straight. It is also important to check the rolls or strips beforehand to make sure the print quality is the same throughout.

Digital wallpaper has the same properties, applications and lifespan as fleece wallpaper, but it is a little more expensive.

Plus points

➕ very individual
➕ wide selection of pictures and designs
➕ can do it yourself if you know how to hang wallpaper
➕ your own photos can be used if the quality is good enough

Minus points

➖ the surface colour must be even and the surface must be smooth, clean and dry
➖ should not be used in areas where there is a lot of contact with the wall, such as the hall or stairs

1 & 2. Existing designs can be chosen or your own ideas developed. 3. The frames are not real. Digital photograph wallpaper has been hung on the wall.

1. Digital photograph wallpaper images can be made of pretty much anything. 2. Personalised living spaces can be created. 3. It does not always have to be a photograph – a quote can also be inspirational.

ACRYLIC
Paint

Paints consist of pigments, a liquid binder and a solvent. The pigments give the paint its colour and opacity, the binder holds everything together and hardens during drying, and the solvent makes sure that the paint is easy to use. The solvent evaporates during drying. There are two main categories of paints: water-based and solvent-based. The second type uses solvents that consist primarily of volatile organic compounds, which have distinctive smells and are also hazardous to health and the environment. They also always need to be thinned with white spirit or turpentine. One such solvent-based paint is alkyd paint, but use of this paint on a large scale is no longer recommended because of its harmful effects.

Latex emulsion paints (generally just called 'emulsion' – see page 161) and acrylic emulsion paints (often just called 'acrylic') are water-based, meaning that the solvent consists primarily of water and the paint can be thinned with water.

Acrylic paints have a pigment with a binding agent of polymer resin and acrylate. They contain more pigment than latex emulsions. Acrylics are available as transparent paints and covering paints. If wood is painted over, the wood grain will always remain visible if a transparent wood dye is used. Transparent lacquers are available in matt, silk and gloss. When choosing a colour, allowance should be made for the fact that the paint will become slightly darker as it dries. Acrylic paint retains its colour well, however, and does not discolour under the influence of UV radiation.

The paint must be stirred thoroughly before use, and the surface dry, clean and undamaged.

It used to be very hard to achieve a smooth result when painting because the brush strokes remained visible, an effect caused by the paint drying so quickly. The quality of acrylics has improved in this respect over recent years: a hard-wearing substance has been added to lengthen the drying time. This gives more time for doing the work, although it also means that it now takes six hours instead of four before a second coat can be applied. There is not much of a problem with odours associated with acrylic paint. Once dry, the paint is moisture-resistant and washable. Acrylic emulsion paint is sometimes used for the bottom coat and then covered with an oil-based paint, but it is difficult to do this the other way round. Painting over acrylic paint is easy. This type of paint is ideal for kitchens but it is better to use vinyl paints in bathrooms.

Plus points
- ✚ wide range of colours and finishes
- ✚ colour-fast
- ✚ short drying time
- ✚ humidity-resistant
- ✚ washable
- ✚ can be painted over

Minus points
- ➖ sometimes gives poor results because of the short drying time

1. This type of paint does resist moisture, but vinyl paint is better for bathrooms. 2. Acrylic paint will not discolour much in UV light.

1. Stripes can be seen more easily with dark colours, so they are harder to apply. 2. The fact that acrylic paint is washable can be very welcome in areas where children play.

EMULSION
Paint

Paints consist of pigments, a liquid binder and a solvent. The pigments give the paint its colour and opacity, the binder holds everything together and hardens during drying, and the solvent makes sure that the paint is easy to use. The solvent evaporates during drying. There are two main categories of paint: water-based and solvent-based. In the latter group, the solvent consists primarily of volatile organic compounds, which have a distinctive odour and are also hazardous to health and the environment. Moreover, they always need to be thinned with white spirit or turpentine. One such solvent-based paint is alkyd paint, but use of this paint on a large scale is no longer recommended because of its harmful effects. Latex and acrylic emulsions (see page 157) are water-based paints, meaning that the solvent consists primarily of water and these paints can be thinned with water.

When using emulsions, the surface must be thoroughly cleaned first and the plasterwork should not be damaged. All dirt and grease must be removed to make sure the paint adheres properly to the wall. The paint will dry in about one hour. Emulsions give a porous coating and preservatives are added to prevent the growth of moulds and bacteria.

Nearly all colours are obtainable in matt, satin and gloss, and this paint is also colour-fast. It is easy to paint over an emulsioned wall in another colour. Washing emulsioned walls is not possible as this paint dissolves in water. This is also the reason why it is better not to use this kind of paint in rooms that are very damp or humid, such as bathrooms. A better option for such rooms is vinyl emulsion, which is similar to normal emulsion but gives improved coverage because it contains more pigment and less calcium carbonate (e.g. lime). It is also porous and can be wiped down, which makes it highly suitable for bathrooms. There are also acrylic/latex emulsions, paints with more pigment and acrylates. This paint is less porous, extremely opaque and ideal for walls that need to be cleaned frequently, such as in the kitchen. Acrylic/latex emulsions are obtainable with a satin finish.

Latex emulsion paints can be found in a range of price categories, with corresponding differences in quality. Note should be taken of the surface area that can be covered with a given pot of paint. More expensive paints often have better coverage properties, which means less paint is required for the same surface area. They are also frequently more environmentally friendly.

Plus points
- ➊ wide range of colours and finishes
- ➊ usually porous
- ➊ resistant to mould and bacteria

Minus points
- ➖ cannot always be washed easily
- ➖ surface must be smooth and clean
- ➖ degree of opacity varies

1. Latex emulsion is porous. 2. As this type of paint cannot be washed with water, it is best in rooms that are not heavily used.

1. More expensive brands of paint often cover better than cheaper ones, so less paint is needed. 2. Vinyl-based emulsions are ideal for more humid rooms.

LIMEWASH
Paint

Ecologically sound building has become an important trend over the last few years, which has boosted interest in working with limewash. This paint is a mixture of natural raw materials, such as slaked lime and water, often with a little white cement added to act as a binding agent. Matt varnish can be used to make the limewash more solid. There are coatings based on lime that give a velvety sheen and there are others that create a marbled effect.

Lime ages attractively and has its own charm. By applying the paint in different ways, a smooth finish or a vivid effect can be created. Limewash can best be applied by a professional as a degree of expertise is required to achieve a good result. Limewash accentuates any irregularities in the wall, and patched areas also remain visible. The surface must be absorbent and not water-repellent. The paint will be dust-free after two or three hours and can be painted over after four hours. This paint often gives off a fine white powder after it has dried, but this problem can be solved by buying limewash containing additives to counteract powdering.

Limewash paints have an antibacterial action and are resistant to moulds. They are also porous, which lets the walls breathe and reduces the chance of moisture problems. Limewash is, therefore, extremely suitable for humid rooms. A top coat of varnish is recommended to make the paint water-resistant and washable. However, this may darken the colour. The paint may also discolour and even weather under the influence of temperature, the underlying surface and air humidity.

Limewash is cheaper than traditional paints.

Plus points
- natural
- porous
- resistant to mould and bacteria
- cheap
- can be painted over after a short time
- suitable for humid rooms

Minus points
- must be applied by professionals
- sometimes gives off a white powder
- not colour-fast
- not very robust
- the surface must be smooth, absorbent and not water-repellent

1. Limewash needs an absorbent substrate. 2. Lively effects can be created, as well as restful ones.

1. Be careful where limewash paint is used – it is vulnerable to greasy fingers! 2. To help make the upkeep easier, a lacquer layer can be applied.

◄ Screen paint reflects the light and is the ideal background for projection.

WALLS   169

SCREEN PAINT
Paint

Projecting images onto a white wall is perfectly possible, but often at the expense of image quality because the clarity and contrast are not as they should be. Using a screen is better, but this always has to be put up or taken down, and is also rather expensive. This problem can now be solved with a specially designed paint – screen paint. This is actually a kind of acrylic emulsion containing small particles that reflect light. A screen-painted projection wall will provide excellent image quality at a high contrast, with good reproduction of the colours. The light reflection takes account of the incidental light at that moment. The screen surface can be made whatever size required and allow for the amount of light in the room.

Screen paint is only available in one colour – white. The paint can be bought in quantities that contain precisely the right amount for the dimensions of the projection surface needed. Certain types of paint produce a screen that is invisible when not in use. It is also possible to paint the entire wall with screen paint, which prevents the edge of the painted screen from being visible during projection. Alternatively, magnetic paint can be used to increase the contrast at the edges. Another option is a magnetic frame, which can be removed after projection has finished.

Applying screen paint requires skill, so it is best to use a professional. The surface must be smooth, dry, firm and clean. A plaster surface should be cement-based. Like any water-based paint, this paint can be thinned with water and it is odourless. Two layers must always be applied using a stainless steel spatula. It is important to work in all directions and to avoid leaving visible spatula tracks. The coating must be scraped down to the grain immediately after applying the paint. Drying times depend on the temperature and air humidity, but the wall is generally touch-dry after four to ten hours and can be painted over (or a second coat applied) after twenty-four hours. The paint can take knocks well and requires little maintenance. It is a durable product, although it is more expensive than the more traditional types of paint.

Plus points
- ➕ handier and more aesthetically pleasing than a projection screen
- ➕ better image quality than an ordinary white wall
- ➕ can be made invisible
- ➕ low maintenance
- ➕ impact-resistant

Minus points
- ➖ is best applied by professionals
- ➖ surface must be smooth, dry, firm and clean
- ➖ expensive

1. This type of paint is only available in white. 2. Direct sunlight on the wall is very annoying; north-facing is ideal.

1

2

1. Try to align the projection, for example as is done with the hearth here. 2. To get the best results, have the screen paint applied by a professional.

PATINA
Paint

Patina has a big effect on the look and ambience of an interior. A patina layer often arises naturally, but there is no need to rely on chance – a piece of furniture or wall can be patinated artificially too. The assortment of decorative paints available offer various alternatives.

Patina paint is a transparent, colourless, acrylic glaze that can be coloured with special pigments for application using decorative paint techniques. The surface must be non-absorbing and have already been painted. A cloth or brush should be used to apply the patina paint, and there will be about an hour during which to create special effects with various techniques. A moist cloth or plastic bag can be crumpled into a ball and pressed into the wet patina. Dabbing – making prints in the wet patina using a flat, hard brush – is another commonly used technique. Special effects can also be created with a sponge: either a little patina is applied to a natural sponge and this is softly dabbed onto the base layer of paint (sponging on), or a layer of patina is applied to the base layer and a natural sponge gently dabbed into the wet patina (sponging off).

The patina layer dries, is durable and water-resistant, and does not yellow or age. The pigments are concentrated and colour-fast. In addition to the basic colours there are shades like emerald and ultramarine, and pigments that give wood effects. Such wood effects are created by applying patina paint containing a wood pigment to a cream-coloured surface and then slowly dragging a wood grain comb or graining rocker through the patina, from the top to the bottom. The colour-fast pigments can also be used to colour varnish.

There are also transparent acrylic glazes available that can be coloured with acrylic or latex paints. These should also be applied to a pre-painted surface, and can be worked with for as long as the paint is wet, which is again about one hour. A tip for creating a stain-resistant lime effect is to use dark blue acrylic paint as a basic layer. A patina should then be made using this dark-blue paint and adding a little white or black. This mixture can be applied to the wall using a broad brush and then the layer immediately brushed over with a dry brush. A natural aging, cracked effect can also be created.

Plus points

+ interesting effects
+ patina creates a certain ambience
+ water-resistant
+ long-lasting result

Minus points

– need to work quickly
– must ask a professional or paint specialist for advice

1. Patinas on large areas are best done by professionals. 2. Limewash gives an attractive weathered effect.

1. Patinating small areas like this hearth is easy enough to do. 2. Make sure that all the requisite materials are to hand. It is a good idea to do a test first on a less visible part.

LOAM OR CLAY PLASTER
Plaster

Loam or clay plaster is one of the oldest building materials. It is a simple, natural raw material made up of fine-grained minerals, and contains sand and clay. The raw materials often come from layers deep below the earth's surface and are, therefore, unpolluted. Loam has been rediscovered over recent years and there has been a lot of research into its building quality. It is available in many colours and structures, has a stylish look and radiates serenity.

Non-professionals with some experience of plastering can apply loam or clay plaster themselves, although this is labour-intensive. The best option is to work with a professional to ensure the plastering is done properly. The same equipment can be used to apply loam as is used to apply other plasterwork. All loose particles should be removed from the surface first to make sure that the plaster adheres properly.

Loam's adhesion strength, sustainability and colour-fastness are important properties. Environmental factors also play a role. Loam is a natural product that can be used largely without chemical additives and can be re-absorbed by nature. It also helps prevent large temperature fluctuations because of its insulating properties. This means that loam plaster stays cool in summer and warm in winter, which in turn helps reduce energy bills.

Loam plaster is moisture-regulating and lets vapour through, creating a healthy indoor climate. The excess moisture in a room is absorbed by the loam, and if the air becomes drier again, the loam will gradually release the moisture back. Loam will, therefore, never result in clammy areas. This type of plaster is also noise-dampening. Loam cannot be used for humid rooms. It is also more fragile than other types of plastering and rather expensive.

Plus points
- ➕ natural
- ➕ healthy
- ➕ durable
- ➕ adheres well
- ➕ colour-fast
- ➕ reduces noise
- ➕ insulating

Minus points
- ➖ is best applied by professionals
- ➖ more fragile than other types of plastering
- ➖ expensive
- ➖ unsuitable for humid rooms

1 | 2 / 3   *1. Loam plaster is very labour-intensive to apply, but has a unique warm radiance. 2. Loam plasters are very stylish and restful. 3. The smoother the finish required, the more labour-intensive the job will be.*

1. Advice from a specialist should be obtained if using a loam or clay plaster in humid rooms. 2. Loam plaster regulates the moisture, insulates and dampens noise. It is an expensive product, but it gives a home a lot of added value.

TADELAKT
Plaster

Tadelakt is a rather unusual product. It is a watertight mixture based on lime, applied using a special technique. It comes from Morocco, where it was originally used mainly for making roofs watertight. These days tadelakt has many different applications – for bathtubs and floors, and also as a wall covering.

The tadelakt technique creates slightly undulating, naturally glossy and very decorative surfaces. Slight differences in emphasis are created and variations in incidental light continually alter the material's appearance. There are a number of basic colours that can be mixed to give the desired colour. Using ochre or iron-oxide red creates an oriental atmosphere.

Tadelakt is best applied by a professional. The mortar is applied to a rough surface in a coat about 5 mm (approx. ¼ in) thick using a spatula. This layer is sanded and polished with a stone the following day until smooth. An olive-based soap layer is placed on top of it, making the wall water-repellent. This creates a glazed tile effect.

Sharp objects and hard knocks can damage tadelakt slightly. Such damage may have its charm and even add value for those who appreciate this touch. The wall should always be cleaned with a special-purpose soap for tadelakt, which ensures that the material stays watertight. Tadelakt is a durable material.

Working with tadelakt is not cheap; application is labour-intensive and as the use of a professional is recommended, costs may become quite high.

Plus points
- ⊕ natural look
- ⊕ moisture-resistant
- ⊕ durable

Minus points
- ⊖ labour-intensive
- ⊖ not very hard-wearing
- ⊖ expensive

1. These four photos show a modern bathroom, with the dark walls in tadelakt to give extra ambience and depth. 2. Although it is a lime-based product, it is completely waterproof because of the special finishing technique that makes it so smooth.

1. Tadelakt creates a calm and natural whole. 2. The material can be used in the kitchen. It is durable and charming, but does have to be applied by a professional.

USED WOOD
Wood

Wood has always been in use as a wall covering. Standard wood types for the interior include pine, whitewood, oak, chestnut, western red cedar, maritime pine and tropical deciduous wood types such as merbau, teak, etc. The wood has to meet a number of specific criteria for use as a wall covering: it must have a certain surface hardness, a balanced moisture content, it should be relatively easy to nail down, and should also require little maintenance. Certain types of wood can be used in humid rooms. Research has shown that the indoor climate is very pleasant when wood is used.

Wood that is several hundred years old can be found for sale. Often it is reclaimed material, from a demolished shed for example. Some producers specialise in importing wood from the Amish in North America or Canada. The Amish are intensely religious people who live in rural communities and reject the modern world. The type of wood they supply, therefore, has a history of its own, which is part of its beauty and charm.

Used wood is processed to make it suitable for reuse. The various types of wood available mean all the natural colour variants are obtainable – grey, red, white, black, etc. Wood also has its own natural design with its lines and grooves. Special techniques can be used to give the wood a hip, modern look: by choosing an opaque finish, by painting it in modern colours, or by smoking, bleaching or cerusing (whitening) the wood. Cerusing involves the wood being sandblasted, after which it is lacquered and sanded. The end result is that the colour is only visible in the grain. Whichever wood is chosen, it is attached to anchor points in the wall.

Wood is durable and noise-dampening. Because of its heat-insulating properties it may also reduce energy costs. Although wood is flammable, the way it burns is slow and predictable and experts say wooden wall coverings pose no greater fire hazard than other materials. An important plus point is that wood is one of the healthiest materials available: it absorbs the humidity in the air and is porous. Wood is also suitable for humid rooms, but a moisture-resistant type needs to be used.

Plus points
- ➕ natural
- ➕ environmentally friendly
- ➕ durable
- ➕ healthy
- ➕ noise-reducing
- ➕ thermally insulating

Minus points
- ➖ not available everywhere
- ➖ expensive

1. Wood insulates and provides a pleasant climate in a home. 2. Old wood has often been around a long time, which has hardened and saturated it, making it withstand moisture better. 3. As a material, used wood adds extra character and cachet to a room.

1
2 | 3

1. The experts say that wooden wall cladding is no more of a fire risk than other wall coverings. 2. Wood in a bathroom should be given a protective coating. 3. Old ships' wood gives a bathroom its own atmosphere.

WALL CORK
Cork

Demand for cork walls has increased massively, largely because of the greater range of colours and textures available. This makes it possible to combine its natural properties with modern designs. Cork comes from the cork oak, which is mainly found in Mediterranean countries. The tree has to be roughly twenty-five years old before its bark is thick enough for cork production. This involves removing a layer of bark from the trunk without damaging the tree, a process that can be repeated every nine years. The older the tree, the better the quality of the cork.

Cork for walls can be purchased in rolls or tiles. Rolls are slightly cheaper but more difficult to apply. There is a high demand for tiles in particular as the range of colours and design options is much greater. Cork is turned into tiles by being boiled, ground and pressed. Cork tiles that retain their shape usually consist of two layers: a base layer made of surplus cork, which determines the quality of the tile, and a thinner layer on top, which determines the look, structure and price of the tile. The average thickness of the tiles is 3 mm ($^1/_8$ in). The natural colour ranges from light beige and soft browns to reddish brown. Coloured tiles include pastel colours, cream and grey. Manufacturers can also produce tiles in any colour, but there is always a slight difference compared with the same paint colour applied to a white surface. Cork is glued onto the wall. Both the cork and the glue should be at room temperature and the room must be warmer than 18°C (64°F) to prevent the glue from drying too slowly. The surface must be entirely smooth, hard and dry. Although cork can be used perfectly well in areas where water is used, the underlying surface must not be moist when applying the cork. The glue must be applied to both the cork and the surface. It is recommended that the joins should be properly sealed if cork is being used in a humid room.

Cork has a number of unique technical characteristics that make it ideal for use as a wall covering. It creates a warm atmosphere and radiates natural simplicity. It is also extremely lightweight, thermally insulating, waterproof, anti-static, durable and noise-reducing. If cork is used as a wall covering in bathrooms, it is recommended that the walls are rinsed and dabbed dry after showering. The cork must also be disinfected occasionally to prevent mould from forming.

Cork is very affordable. Wall cork costs no more than floor cork, but the processing is more expensive.

Plus points
- ➕ user-friendly
- ➕ wide range of colours and patterns
- ➕ natural
- ➕ noise-reducing
- ➕ moisture-resistant
- ➕ anti-static
- ➕ durable

Minus points
- ➖ the processing (as opposed to the material itself) is rather expensive
- ➖ scarce resource
- ➖ requires maintenance and disinfecting when used in bathrooms

1. Accentuating a wall with a cork covering is an original solution. 2. It is a material that gives a bedroom a warm and cosy feeling. 3. Cork can even be used almost like ceramic tiles.

1 | 2 / 3   *1. This material is also well-suited for use in bathrooms, but does require more upkeep than standard ceramic tiles. 2. Cork does not reflect sound well, so it helps create a more restful living or working environment. 3. These four different shades are part of the unlimited range of available colours.*

WALL LAMINATE
Laminate

There has been a considerable increase in the use of laminate over recent years, not just for flooring but for walls as well. Laminate is based on HDF sheeting, which is made of fine wood fibres that have been compressed to a high density and glued to make them watertight. The more the fibres are compressed, the better the quality. A pattern layer (a photo print) is placed on top with a transparent melamine coating on top of that.

For a long time laminate was considered to be a rather second-rate, imitation product, but the improvements in quality have now put it among the high-end materials, both technically and aesthetically. Laminate can hardly be distinguished from real wood these days and often even has a wood-like 'grain'. Moreover, manufacturers are responding to the demand for original designs and creative applications. Transparent laminates with three-dimensional effects or with a screen print or a digital print, are all obtainable. Any pattern or optical effect can be produced, with the original image being reproduced realistically in high-quality colours. Laminate is often used as a wall covering in combination with other materials or for carefully chosen areas. It is generally unsuitable for humid areas as the fibre sheet may absorb moisture. However, there is a thicker type of laminate using reinforced paper (Kraft paper) impregnated with phenolic resin, which is suitable for such areas and is, therefore, frequently used in showers and toilets. It can take aggressive cleaning agents and disinfecting products well. Laminate with a Kraft paper core must not be mounted on the wall directly, but should be placed on a grid to allow the material to expand and shrink. It is important to call in a professional if installing this type of laminate.

Because laminate has the look of wood it creates the same warm, natural effect. This material is colour-fast and resistant to sunlight. It is also very tough, hard-wearing and easy to maintain. Water and everyday cleaning products are all that are required. Moist microfibre cloths or chamois ('shammy') leather should always be used, as scouring pads or scouring agents may cause scratches.

Laminate is cheaper than real wood.

Plus points
- ⊕ hard-wearing
- ⊕ durable
- ⊕ wide range of colours and patterns
- ⊕ low maintenance
- ⊕ cheaper than wood
- ⊕ colour-fast

Minus points
- ⊖ artificial
- ⊖ quality is variable
- ⊖ some types are unsuitable for humid areas

1. A full-wall wardrobe made of laminate is cheaper than a solid wooden version. 2. Laminate is very tough and low maintenance, so it is ideal for kitchens. 3. Even perforated finishes are possible.

1. Cupboards and drawers can be integrated invisibly into the wall. 2. This is not an everyday headboard. 3. This bathroom uses a moisture-resistant laminate with a dark zebrawood finish.

BAS-RELIEF IMAGES
Vector technology

It was not until the 1990s that methods were discovered for using images in milling and grinding programmes. This was done using vector technology. Mathematical descriptors called vectors allow images to be milled into all kinds of sheet materials, such as wood, metal or stone. A milling machine cuts the pattern into the material, with the contrast between the colour of the grooves and the colour of the sheet surface creating the image.

The material being milled plays an important part in the effect created. The contrast becomes sharper and clearer depending on the coloration, which enables specific moods or effects to be achieved: for example, a serene wall covering or a strong, eye-catching image. Concrete can also be used as the base material.

Any image can be reproduced down to the last detail – photos, children's drawings, paintings, logos, abstract designs. It is also possible to play with the size of the image. Of course, it is a good idea to take the layout of the room and the interior into account; multiple sheets sometimes have to be used for larger images.

This technique has been refined over the years and a global patent has been obtained for it. It is still a technique that requires considerable experience, however, and the best option is to have the image installed by a professional. The method used to put it up will depend on the material used for milling.

Dust can accumulate in the grooves so regular cleaning is required. A wall containing a bas-relief image is not cheap, but the images are durable.

Plus points
- ➕ very exclusive
- ➕ a wide selection of images
- ➕ durable

Minus points
- ➖ expensive
- ➖ not dust-free, as there is always a relief pattern
- ➖ must be installed by professionals

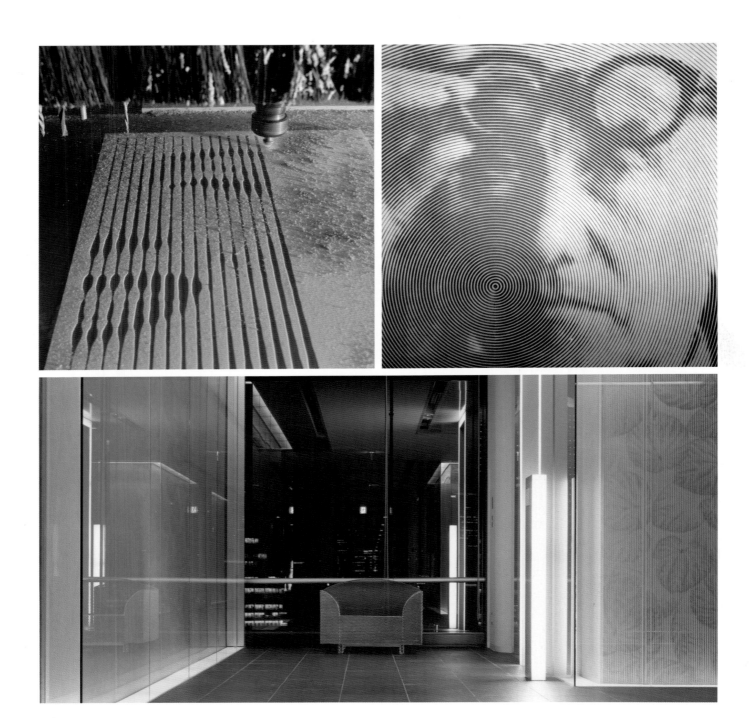

1 | 2

3

1. Images can be milled into wood, concrete or metal. 2. The incidental light plays a major role in how the image is seen. 3. The main applications for bas-relief images are in the business market.

1. The table and the chairs have the same milled image. 2. An example of how the lighting angle creates the image. 3. This is a very expensive technique, but it makes every item of furnishing unique.

◀ *Authentic ceiling ornaments are often restored or replaced using plastic versions because these are cheaper and easier to fit.*

WALLS   201

PLASTIC
Cornices

An attractive, and relatively simple, solution to give a room a new look without wallpapering or painting it again is to place cornices in the corners where the walls meet the ceiling. It is possible nowadays to buy cornices that can simply be glued in place. These are often made from duro-polymers, an unbreakable raw material that is easily painted over.

To go a step further, matching decorative wall lighting can be chosen. This allows features to be picked out, giving the room a character of its own. Other options include decorating the mantelpiece or creating a horizontal strip (skirting board) at the bottom of the wall.

The cornices should be brought to room temperature for twenty-four hours beforehand, as there must not be any large differences in temperature or air humidity when they are fitted. Measures also need to be taken to prevent bright sunlight from shining onto the cornices during installation. The cornice pieces have rough surfaces designed to take the adhesive well and they can easily be glued into position using a specially developed water-soluble paste. This is available in containers and is best applied with a spray gun, which can also be used for sealing the joins. Paste residues are simple to remove because they dissolve in water. Once installed, the cornices can be painted over. Ordinary wall paint can be used and there is no need for a primer as the cornice pieces will generally have already been primed.

The material used for cornices is reasonably hard and, therefore, impact-resistant. Cornices are rather expensive.

Plus points
⊕ easy to install
⊕ can be painted over
⊕ decorative
⊕ durable
⊕ impact-resistant

Minus points
⊖ expensive
⊖ not UV-resistant

1. A wide range of plastic cornices are available. 2. Less grandiose cornices also add a nice finishing touch to a modern home.

1. The ceiling lighting accentuates the cornices. 2. The lightweight structure makes cornicing easier to fit than plasterwork. 3. The photos on the right show the broad spectrum of applications possible: the material can be used as wainscot panels, wall decoration or for concealing indirect, atmospheric lighting.

1
2 3

◄ *There are numerous types of natural stone wall cladding. Grey slate is very popular again.*

WALLS   205

NATURAL STONE
Stone

The earth's crust consists largely of natural stone. It is rare to find two stone beds exactly the same, as the processes that create natural rock and the geological properties are all so different. Natural stone types with a similar composition are classed in the same group. There are solidified (igneous) rocks, such as basalt and granite, and deposited (sedimentary) rocks, such as limestone, sandstone and slate. Large blocks of stone are cut from the rock in stone quarries and sawn into sheets or slabs.

Natural stone tiles can be mortared or glued (cemented) into position. If mortar is used the wall needs three months to dry out, and as little water as possible should be used during that period. A cemented wall will be completely dry within a month. Natural stone can be finished in many different ways. Polishing involves the stone's surface being sanded, which makes it shine and reinforces the colours. Honing means the stone is gently sanded while being sprayed with water until semi-matt and smooth. Other finishes are somewhat more irregular, which makes the colours dull and leaves the surface rough. This is the case when the stone is granulated (processed with a special hammer, sometimes known as a 'bush hammer') or flamed.

The variations in composition mean each type of natural stone has different properties, which will also affect the type of upkeep work that is needed. In general, cleaning the stones with a moist cloth is recommended. For more information about specific types of natural stone, please see 'Floors' on pages 99 to 121.

Natural stone is the basis for the innovative material Stoneskin®. The crust and edge slices of natural stone slabs are cut into fine strips and bonded with polyester resin into a sheet of approximately 60 x 15 cm (24 x 6 in) which provides a realistic result. The sheets can be installed easily with special adhesive cement. Once the material has dried fully, it should be treated with a special product to bring out its colour and structure. There are various products available and the most suitable will depend on the particular type of natural stone used to make the Stoneskin®. The salesperson should be asked for advice. Maintenance is easy: regular dusting is all that is required, although specific cleaning agents are also obtainable.

Plus points
+ wide choice of colours, finishes and designs
+ natural

Minus points
– must be installed by professionals
– expensive

1. Narrow vertical stone tiles add height to the room. 2. If the budget allows, extending the floor covering into the walls can look impressive.

1 2 3

1. *Various sizes of tile can be used together on a single wall. 2. Natural materials always give a room a luxurious look. 3. Natural materials generally attract more dust than synthetics.*

TRANSLUCENT CONCRETE
Concrete

One of the most recent and astonishing developments in materials is the advent of translucent concrete. Concrete, the archetypical hard, impenetrable material, is given a translucent effect by embedding glass fibres in it. These transparent synthetic fibres create a new experience. Light is literally allowed to pass from one side of the wall to the other, so that the rather dark, heavy feeling of conventional concrete is converted into light, airy designs. Translucent concrete is also available using recycled glass.

Translucent concrete is delivered in prefabricated blocks and then polished. It is available in pale beige, light grey and dark grey, and with an organic or layered scattering pattern. The blocks can be manufactured in various sizes and are thermally insulating. The blocks can be stacked on top of each other and glued together with two-component cement. If desired, joints can be filled with mortar of the same colour as the blocks.

Translucent concrete appears less thick and heavy than traditional concrete, but that is an illusion. In fact, translucent concrete retains the same strength and durability as traditional concrete and it can, therefore, be used in a similar way in load-bearing elements. This is because the proportion of glass fibres is fairly low and their diameter small.

The thickness of the fibres ranges between 2 micrometres and two millimetres (under a thousandth of an inch to $1/10$ in). The different diameters give different effects, with thin fibres creating a rather diffuse impression whereas thicker fibres can be used to generate a specific image, such as a logo.

The blocks are heat-resistant and temperature effects will not crack them. Translucent concrete is easy to maintain: dry or wet cleaning on a regular basis will suffice, although some materials (such as mineral greases, oils or acids) may leave indelible stains. The product itself is still rather expensive, but the production techniques are constantly being improved. This should mean that installing it will become significantly more straightforward and, therefore, cheaper in the future.

Plus points
- ➕ innovative
- ➕ translucent, airy effect
- ➕ all the pluses of concrete
- ➕ heat-resistant
- ➕ low maintenance

Minus points
- ➖ expensive
- ➖ must be installed by professionals
- ➖ hard to obtain
- ➖ certain materials may leave indelible stains

1	2
3	4

1. Translucent concrete is a new and original material. 2. This type of concrete can also be used for load-bearing walls in houses. 3. Close up, the fibres that transmit the light can be seen. 4. The thicker the concrete, the less light gets through.

1. Translucent concrete is unique and durable, but some stains and marks can affect the material. 2. Its versatility allows it to be used in all sorts of creative ways. 3. The blocks have been put in a frame here, rather than cemented: the material in its purest form.

CERAMIC TILES
Ceramics

Ceramic tiles are made from finely ground clay that is compressed into shape at high pressure and then baked at high temperatures. Glazed ceramic tiles have a coloured glazed upper layer, which gives a choice of colours, glossiness, decorations and designs. Unglazed tiles usually have no decorations or patterns.

The compactness of the tiles may also differ: they may be impermeable, or the pores may be interconnected. The more porous the tiles are, the greater their capacity for absorbing moisture. The tile colour depends on the raw materials used, although colour pigments can be added in certain cases.

Ceramic tiles are hard, durable, non-flammable, tough and hygienic. Fully glazed tiles can withstand frost. They are watertight and do not stain, so they require very little upkeep. All that is needed is cleaning with hot water and a cleaning agent, followed by rinsing with clean water.

For more information about the common types of ceramic tiles see page 87.

A new generation of ceramic tiles is now becoming increasingly popular: barely 3 mm thick (approx. $\frac{1}{8}$ in) and available in relatively large sizes, e.g. 1 x 3 m (39 x 117 in). These tiles are hard-wearing and resistant to the effects of bright light, and they also retain their shine. Because the sheets are so thin, they can be cut easily with a glass cutter or a normal cutting machine. When tiles are used on walls, cut-aways often have to be made for sockets, drains or light fittings and the latest generation of tiles takes this into account. The requisite cutaway can be made using a grinder or a hollow milling cutter before the tile is applied to the wall. Furthermore, these innovative thinner tiles are easier to install and, because they weigh less, they are well-suited for use on plasterboard walls. The underlying surface does not have to be treated with a special product, although it does still need to be smooth. Another advantage is that the number of joints can be limited and the few joints still required can be kept very narrow, which improves hygiene because dirt cannot accumulate in them. These tiles are, therefore, excellent for use in bathrooms or toilets.

Plus points
- ✚ wide range of colours, designs, sizes, shapes and structures
- ✚ hard-wearing
- ✚ durable
- ✚ do not stain
- ✚ moisture-resistant
- ✚ very low maintenance

Minus points
- ➖ must be put in place by professionals
- ➖ price and quality may vary a great deal

1. Ceramic tiles are low-maintenance: very suitable for kitchens and bathrooms. 2. The latest generation of tiles are only 3 mm (¹/8 in) thick, light enough for plasterboard walls. 3. Glazed tiles give mirror reflections.

1. These small matt tiles are available in various sizes and dozens of colours. 2. This kitchen wall is tiled with zelliges, hand-made glazed Moroccan tiles. 3. Terracotta tiles are used here. They are usually enamelled and their final size varies.

MOSAICS
Mosaics

Mosaics consist of small blocks or pieces of hard material such as marble, stone, plain or coloured glass, stainless steel, terracotta or ceramics, that are laid in patterns and cemented in place.

Mosaic stones have been used in bathrooms and kitchens since antiquity. Their versatility is the reason why they are now being used increasingly for other interior walls. There are various materials, designs and colours that can be combined in different ways. Glass mosaic pieces are available in various designs (matt, mother-of-pearl and translucent) and more than a hundred colours, but usually only one size, 1.5 x 1.5 cm (approx. ½ x ½ in). Ceramic mosaic pieces are available in multiple sizes and a large number of different colours. About forty different types of marble mosaic blocks are available. There are smoothly polished pieces that can be used to create a designer look, while other pieces are somewhat rough and have a natural stone look. There is, therefore, plenty of scope for producing a highly individual effect. Creating accents with mosaics is a growing trend, for example by adding a narrow horizontal or vertical strip. This allows lively elements to be added, or alternatively soothing patterns to be introduced.

Professional help is recommended if you want to install a mosaic. Installation used to be a complex and labour-intensive process, but nowadays much of the material is prefabricated. Although the patterns are still made by hand, they can be arranged beforehand and stuck onto nets, which in turn can be cut into variable shapes. These are then usually put in place as just a few large composite pieces using tile adhesive, a mortar glue that is applied to both the wall and the tiles. The underlying surface must be dry, smooth and dust-free. The right information should be obtained about the best filler (grouting) to use for the joins between the tiles. Too much moisture can cause mould that is often very hard to get rid of and using a two-component grout can avoid a lot of serious problems. Mosaics have the same characteristics as the materials they are made of in terms of moisture resistance, temperature sensitivity, abrasion resistance and so forth. The maintenance of the wall also depends on the material used. Marble mosaics must be cleaned in the same way as natural stone (see page 205), whereas glass mosaics only need soap and water.

Mosaics are rather expensive, but can also be used for a smaller surface area as a detail.

Plus points
- ⊕ wide range of colours, designs, sizes, shapes and structures
- ⊕ the same plus points as the material that the mosaic pieces are made from

Minus points
- ⊖ expensive
- ⊖ must be installed by professionals
- ⊖ the same minus points as the material that the mosaic pieces are made from

1. One possibility for mosaic tiles is shown here, but the variations are limitless. 2. The smaller the pieces, the harder they are to place and professional advice should be sought. 3. The basin can also be tiled with a mosaic.

1. To create a graduation from light to dark, the stones have to be placed individually. 2. Mosaics are generally obtainable on net mats, making it easier to install. 3. A mosaic is great for truly creative applications.

GLASS WALLS
Glass

Glass walls are widely used, in particular as separating walls. Working with glass creates a livelier, lighter impression than a full wall. The degree of privacy and the extent to which the wall is transparent can be determined according to individual requirements. There are also a large number of options for optical effects. For example, mirrored glass reflects the light and makes the room look larger, as well as creating depth.

Mirrored glass is available in an environmentally-friendly variant that does not contain copper or lead but instead has a silver base with a protective coating on top. The glass for glass walls is obtainable in numerous variations. Sand-blasted glass has a matt look created by the friction of the grains, and this effect can be used to etch an image or lined pattern into the glass. Lacquered glass is glossy, which creates an aesthetic and highly modern effect. The lacquer, which is also environmentally friendly and long-lasting, is applied to the back of the glass so that the colour remains intact and the paint cannot get scratched. This will also retain the shine of the glass. The other side of the glass is de-lustred with an acid to give it a satin look. An entire wall can be covered with glass panels or just a few used for decorative emphasis.

It is best to call in a professional for the installation of a glass wall.

Glass is durable and (because it is so smooth) upkeep is easy. Lacquered glass is resistant to aggressive cleaning agents. It is important to obtain proper information about the material being worked with. Factors to take into account include acoustics, thermal insulation and safety aspects. The glass is often covered with foil to protect against scratches and to make sure that any splinters stick to the foil if the glass breaks. Corners of panes are particularly vulnerable, especially if the pane of glass is not mounted on a support such as a wooden frame.

Plus points

➕ wide selection of glass types, patterns and finishes

➕ light and airy

➕ can also act as a protective, transparant covering

➕ low maintenance

Minus points

➖ must be installed by professionals

1. Frosted and clear glass are available in all RAL (NCS) colours. 2. Coloured glass can be perfect as a separating wall in a bathroom.

1	2
3	4

1. *Glass tiles have been around since the Sixties, and are now experiencing a real revival. 2. Glass can also be cemented to the wall. 3. Semi-transparent glass provides privacy and still lets enough light through. 4. The three photos, bottom right: laminated glass is used in the interior because it is much safer.*

KITCHENS

◄ *Various kitchen layouts can be considered. A kitchen 'island' is always an eye-catcher.*

KITCHENS 227

KITCHEN LAYOUT
A few possibilities

The layout chosen for a kitchen is very important because the equipment and furniture can be positioned in many different ways. Account needs to be taken of the available space and the location of the kitchen, and allowance also made for the doors and windows and the positioning of the ducts for electricity, water and gas. If the kitchen is a room everyone passes through to go to the garden then it is better to choose a safe layout where hot water does not need to be carried from one side of the room to the other.

In particular, thought should be given beforehand to whether an open or closed kitchen is wanted. In an open kitchen everything is visible to visitors and it may, therefore, be handy to be able to clear things away quickly.

Although any layout will permit the use of a wide selection of materials, account should still be taken of the layout as certain materials may work better than others. As is difficult to camouflage a cooking hood over a central cooking range, it is better to choose an attractive cooking hood or, alternatively, one with edge extraction which can be built into the ceiling. If the layout is short of space, it is better to be sparing in the use of materials.

The parallel kitchen makes optimum use of the space. It is the favourite layout in professional kitchens because there is plenty of space to move around in. All cupboards and equipment are placed in two parallel rows to make sure that everything is within reach. There is also plenty of storage. The space between the rows must be wide enough to allow the cupboards and drawers on both sides to be opened at the same time.

This layout is not recommended if people are frequently passing through the kitchen and certainly not if the gap between the sides is too narrow. After all, this could lead to dangerous situations, for example when someone is moving from one side to the other carrying hot pans.

The central cooking range or 'island' is becoming extremely popular. In this layout various items of equipment and kitchen furniture are placed in a group in the middle. Usually, the island is the central point in the kitchen – an eye-catcher.

It often overlooks the dining area so that people in the kitchen can easily follow conversations. Some designs will make it possible to place a few bar stools in the kitchen to allow breakfast or light meals to be served there.

In an island kitchen useful items can be stored in racks hanging from the ceiling, so that there is hardly any walking involved. Care should be taken in the design, however, to ensure that there is still plenty of room to move around.

Gas pipes and electricity cables must be installed at an early stage. This type of kitchen is also known as a 'living kitchen'.

In a single-wall kitchen, everything is arranged in a line. This is ideal for narrow or small rooms, although a full wall of at least 3 m (10 ft) with no windows or doors is required. Compromises often have to be made because of the lack of space. Consideration needs to be given to items and equipment which are required most often, and to how these can be stored efficiently. The worktop is usually not that large in this layout.

An L-shaped kitchen (two sides of a square room) often creates an open feel with plenty of space. A table and chairs can usually

1. This parallel kitchen layout is the most user-friendly set-up. 2. A single-wall kitchen means that the cook's back is towards everyone else.

1 & 2. Two kitchen islands, one modern and one in a more traditional style.

1
—
2

KITCHEN LAYOUT (CONTINUED)
A few possibilities

be placed in it, which is nice and sociable if a lot of time is spent in the kitchen. Two adjacent walls are used, which means there is no through passage and a lot of worktop space can be created. The most important kitchen appliances should all be placed in a corner as this reduces the walking distance to a minimum. The storage space for the items required less often should be put at the ends of the kitchen.

In U-shaped kitchens use is made of three walls, which creates a lot of space for cooking and storage.

This layout is only recommended for large kitchens as the dining table can be placed in the middle. If this is done when there is not much free space it will create a feeling of being hemmed in. Too little space can also be inconvenient if cooking with a group of people is important, although there is the advantage that everything is within easy reach.

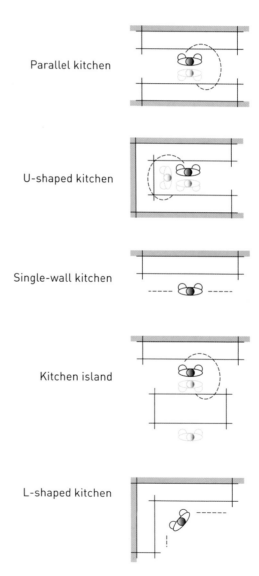

Parallel kitchen

U-shaped kitchen

Single-wall kitchen

Kitchen island

L-shaped kitchen

Both traditional and modern U-shaped kitchens utilise three walls.

1. There is plenty of room for a dining table in the middle. 2. An L-shaped kitchen with non-fitted furniture.

ERGONOMICS
Practical hints

The distance between the dining table and kitchen can be covered more than thirty times a day, and drawers, cupboards and doors opened and closed eighty times a day. Preparing food, cooking and clearing up – all involve walking, stopping, lifting, bending down, etc. A practical, comfortable kitchen can make all the difference, which is why ergonomics should play a key role when designing. The work triangle concept was developed more than fifty years ago. It links the three most important locations: the storage space, the area where preparation – including washing – takes place, and the place for the actual cooking. Walking and moving around this triangle should be optimised. The Blum Company expanded the 'work triangle' model into a theory based on five zones:

(1) There is a food storage or larder zone for stored food and refrigerated groceries. It is handy to have these close together so that your ingredients don't have to be collected from all corners of the kitchen.

(2) The utility storage zone takes up most space. It contains the glasses, cutlery, crockery and other kitchen utensils like plastic containers.

(3) Cutting boards, knives, herbs and other accessories are stored in the preparation zone. The best location for this zone is between the cooking zone and washing-up zone.

(4) The sink and the dishwasher are placed in the washing-up zone. This is the ideal location for dishcloths, hand soap, cleaning agents, small dustbins and polishing materials.

(5) The extraction hood, oven, pots and pans, collection of spices and kitchen implements should be in the cooking zone.

It is important to take these five zones into account during the initial design of the kitchen. Everything belonging to one zone should be placed close together to avoid having to walk back and forth frequently and unnecessarily. It is also important to consider the sequence of the zones, for example a layout from left (1) to right (5) is the most efficient for right-handed people, while from right (5) to left (1) is more appropriate for left-handed people. Finally, personal requirements should be considered. The storage space needed will depend on lifestyle and cooking habits, and may change in the course of time, for instance with the arrival of children. It is important, therefore, to make sure there is enough storage space.

Not only is a functional layout needed in a kitchen, but efficiency also needs to be considered when choosing kitchen elements. The height of the worktop in particular is important. This can be chosen to suit a person's height. The depth should be approx. 60 cm (24 in) so that items can be reached easily. The oven needs to be operated without too much difficulty and should be placed at a handy height. For safety reasons the oven should definitely not be installed too high up: 1.3 metres (4 ft) between the floor and the bottom of the oven is the maximum. It is better not to use doors for the lower cupboards because this means having to bend down to take something out of the back. Working with drawers will be easier and gives an overview of the contents.

When cupboards are placed high up, it can be a good idea to give them interior drawers or slides. Everything will then be within reach and nicely arranged, and the entire contents won't need to be taken out every time something is required. The drawers and cupboards should have a practical, clear layout. If necessary, shelves and partitions can be used with adjustable width and height. It is important that drawers can be pulled out to their full extent and that they have high walls at the sides

1. As it is easier to see into drawers they are more ergonomic than cupboards with doors. 2. Drawers with open/close mechanisms make less noise and last longer.

1. It is better to put fragile items such as glassware in cupboards that are higher up. 2. A practical kitchen layout helps keep walking distances down to a minimum.

ERGONOMICS (CONTINUED)
Practical hints

and back so that equipment can be piled up without it falling out. Upper cupboards should be able to open through a wide angle as that makes it easier to remove items.

Ways should always be found to try to make optimum use of the available space in a kitchen, otherwise a lot of space could be wasted in the corners or under the sink. It is also important to store the items used most as close as possible to the worktop. Cutlery is often required so it is best to put this in a drawer just below the worktop. The lower shelves of the upper cupboards are also a suitable location as they are within easy reach as well. Items that are not used often should be placed on the highest shelves or in the bottom drawers.

In summary, when planning a kitchen it is worth paying attention not only to the aesthetic aspects but also to the functional ones. This will save a lot of time and energy in day-to-day activities.

1 & 2. Drawers with cutlery and utensils are best placed as close as possible to the preparation zone.

1 & 2. Low down cupboards that contain drawers of various sizes make the kitchen much easier to use.

◄ The worktop defines the appearance of the kitchen to a large extent. The coloured patterning of veined marble gives this kitchen its look and feel.

KITCHENS   243

MARBLE
Stone worktops

Marble is the result of metamorphosis of limestone at very high pressures and temperatures. The fossils that can be found in limestone are no longer recognisable in the marble. Marble is light coloured and often has veins of yellow, brown or grey, natural colour nuances and a crystalline structure. The veins that are sometimes found in marble are the result of impurities in the limestone.

Tumbled marble is treated with a product after processing that gives the stone an antique and more natural look. The surface of tumbled marble is less smooth than other types. Marble for worktops is sometimes honed as well, giving it a silky sheen.

A marble worktop must be fitted by a professional. Up to a certain size, it is possible to make worktops as a single piece. If not, several slabs will be fitted next to each other, which means that a small joint will be visible. It is also possible to integrate a marble sink, in which case the joint will be glued.

Marble feels cold and smooth, but is softer than granite. It is only heat-resistant up to a certain extent and is susceptible to scratching, which is why only top-quality marble is recommended for use in the kitchen. Marble is classified into four categories: Class A being the top quality and Class D the lowest. The worktop must be treated regularly with a sealant as marble absorbs water and oils easily. Sealing is particularly important for honed marble. This treatment also protects the marble against damage by acids.

The best cleansers for maintenance are hot water and a neutral soap.

Marble is a rather expensive material.

Plus points
+ natural look

Minus points
- must be installed by professionals
- expensive
- must be treated with a sealant
- not scratch-resistant
- only heat-resistant to a certain extent

1. Carrara marble comes into its own in modern kitchens. 2. There are all sorts of ways of finishing natural stone.

1. Marble is available in four classes: from A (the best quality) to D (the lowest). 2. These two photos show sinks built in underneath the worktop. The sink can be in the same material or made of stainless steel.

BASALT
Stone worktops

Basalt is a volcanic igneous rock that is formed when lava cools. Because the lava cools down relatively quickly, no large crystals are formed, which gives the stone the fine-grained structure that typifies its aesthetic appeal. Basalt typically has light colour nuances on a dark-grey background and is the darkest of all natural stones. Most variants are not at all porous and very hard, which makes this stone highly suitable as a kitchen worktop.

A basalt worktop must be installed by a professional. Up to a certain size, it is possible to make worktops as a single piece. If not, several slabs will be fitted next to each other, which means that a small joint will be visible. It is also possible to integrate a basalt sink, with a cemented joint. Most basalt worktops are honed, which gives them a silky sheen although it also means any stains on the surface are more easily visible.

The stone is very hard and can take a few knocks in the kitchen. Hot pots and pans can be placed on the worktop as basalt is resistant to heat. This type of stone also does not scratch easily, and it is hard-wearing and durable. It is hardly affected by stains because it is so dense and has very few pores, and acids will not leave marks either. Even so, the best way to protect the stone is by using a sealant. If a glossy variant has been chosen and the stone has turned slightly matt over the course of time, a shining agent can be used to make it gleam again. There are also cleaning agents for persistent dirt, but soap and water will be sufficient for day-to-day cleaning.

Basalt is one of the more expensive natural stones because of its high quality and durability.

Plus points
- ➕ hard
- ➕ durable
- ➕ not very porous
- ➕ scratch-resistant
- ➕ acid-resistant
- ➕ heat-resistant
- ➕ low maintenance

Minus points
- ➖ must be installed by professionals
- ➖ expensive

1. Having the floor and the worktop made of the same material creates a uniform whole. 2. This is a good example of a sunken basin made of the same material as the worktop. The edges of the sink are glued together.

1
2 | 3

1. Basalt has been used in a more traditional kitchen here. 2. Basalt does not always have to be black. 3. The splash wall can be made in the same material as well but, if so, a hard and stain-resistant natural stone should be chosen, as was done here.

GRANITE
Stone worktops

Granite, along with stainless steel (see page 279), is one of the best materials for worktops as it is all but indestructible. Granite consists primarily of three minerals: coloured feldspar, grey quartz and black biotite. These minerals had enough time to form crystals during the granite's very slow process of cooling down, which explains the stone's speckled appearance. Granite is obtainable in various colours and also in matt or glossy designs.

The worktop must be installed by professionals. Up to a certain size, it is possible to make worktops as a single piece. If not, several slabs will be fitted next to each other, which means that a small joint will be visible. It is also possible to integrate a granite sink using a cemented joint. If desired, a granite splash wall can also be made, which creates an attractive look. Granite worktops are usually polished, which gives them a shiny surface but also means any scratches are easily visible. These can be removed by re-polishing the worktop.

Granite is very durable – the stone is hard, does not scratch easily and is heat-resistant. Hot cooking pans can be left on it to cool, but pans must not be too hot as the difference in temperature could cause cracks. A cutting board should always be used to protect the worktop. Granite is non-porous, but should be treated regularly with a special product to give the stone even better protection against permeating moisture. It can be easily cleaned with soap and water, but cleaning with abrasives is not recommended. Granite is resistant to acids, such as those in citrus fruits or vinegar, but persistent stains, such as from red wine or red beetroots, must be wiped off immediately. In the course of time the granite's shine could become more matt, but regular maintenance of the worktop will restrict this. Granite is an expensive type of stone.

A cheaper alternative is granulated stone, made of ground granite granules. This stone is hard-wearing, and resistant to scratches and high temperatures. Marble is sometimes sold as granite. To test a stone, a small scratch should be made at an inconspicuous location using a sharp knife. If the scratch is white and powdery, the material could well be marble.

Plus points
- ✚ wide range of colours
- ✚ heat-resistant
- ✚ scratch-resistant
- ✚ durable
- ✚ usually acid-resistant
- ✚ low maintenance

Minus points
- ➖ must be installed by professionals
- ➖ expensive

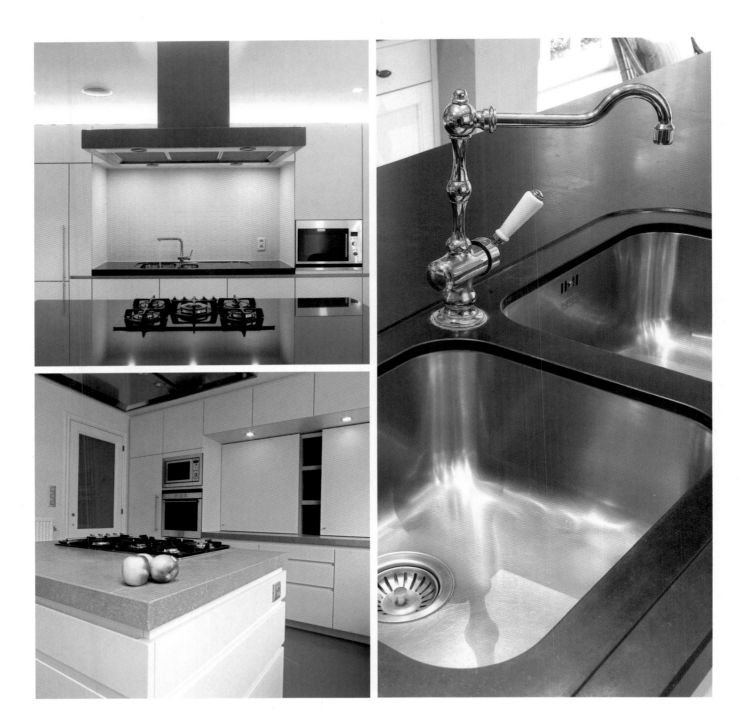

1. These two photos show the difference between polished and unpolished granite. Unpolished granite is more liable to stain. 2. Granite can be milled beautifully into shape, as can be seen in the subtle transition to the sinks here.

1. Even though granite is heat-resistant, care should always be taken with hot pans. 2. The material can withstand the acids in citrus and other fruits. 3. Granite does not scratch at all easily.

BLUESTONE
Stone worktops

A variety of types of stone go under the name 'bluestone' but, with the exception of some American sandstones, they are all compact, dark types of limestone that may contain fossil remnants, such as petrified molluscs and plants. Depending on the finish, the colour ranges from light grey to dark blue-grey. Belgian bluestone in particular is very popular, although Asian variants are increasingly being used. Both types have similar origins, composition and properties. However, Chinese bluestone contains a lot of dolomite, which may give it a brown glaze after a while. It also contains fewer fossils and the colour is not as deep. The quality is often inferior to Belgian bluestone. A bluestone worktop must be fitted by a professional. Up to a certain size, it is possible to make worktops as a single piece. If not, several slabs will be fitted next to each other, which means that a small joint will be visible. It is also possible to integrate a bluestone sink with a cemented joint. Because this natural stone scratches more easily than other types, the worktops are usually honed, which gives bluestone a silky sheen. Bluestone is fairly hard, but rather porous at the same time. Although the stone scratches easily, these scratches can be removed simply enough with a special scouring pad. Bluestone is sensitive to acids because of the high proportion of calcium carbonate contained in the stone; soft drinks or juices made from citrus fruits can, therefore, leave stains. If an acid product is spilt on the stone, it should be wiped off with an oil-soaked cloth to give the stone additional protection in that spot.

Bluestone can be treated with a sealant to reduce the effect of stains. The best method is to use a fifty-fifty mixture of linseed oil and turpentine. Even so, it is never possible to prevent staining entirely and this will eventually give the stone an unusual patina.

Bluestone offers excellent value for money.

Plus points
- ⊕ durable
- ⊕ good value for money

Minus points
- ⊖ porous
- ⊖ scratches easily
- ⊖ affected by acids
- ⊖ can stain
- ⊖ must be treated with a sealing agent

1. A honed worktop is less susceptible to staining. 2. Bluestone is the perfect stone for a cosy kitchen with a rustic feel.

1. The photos left and bottom: a chopping board should be used as bluestone scratches quite easily. The top photo shows an original solution. 2. These four photos clearly show the special look that bluestone can provide.

COMPOSITE STONE
Worktops

The name says it all: a composite stone is made artificially from a mixture of materials. Residues of granite, marble, glass or quartz are ground and often mixed with a plastic. This gives the stone a less natural look than pure natural stone, but the result is a very strong material with a long life. Almost any colour or pattern is available. There are glossy and matt designs, depending on the finish of the stone: brushed (a rough surface), polished or honed. Scratches are more easily visible on a polished surface. The range of different finishes mean composite stone can be used in all interiors. It is often used in combination with stainless steel.

Composite stone can be purchased in a standard size or a worktop cut to size. Separate parts are fitted in place with an invisible joint. If the sink is to be made from the same material, no joints will be needed.

The quality and price of composite stone depends on the composition. The material it is made of will affect how susceptible it is to scratches, how well it resists heat and how hard-wearing the kitchen worktop is. For example, composite stone based on granite or quartz is scratch-free, hard-wearing and acid-resistant. All types of composite stone are resistant to stains and moisture, as well as being easy to maintain - all that is needed is soap and water. Aggressive cleaning agents should never be used. Stains and fingerprints are easily visible on honed worktops, so to prevent this the worktop should be treated with a special product, polishing the stone with it several times if necessary. In the course of time the worktop will be saturated from cleaning with standard domestic products and, as a result, stains will no longer be formed. The smooth surface gives moulds and bacteria less chance to grow because they cannot accumulate in small holes and grooves. Even so, a composite worktop will generally require cleaning with a special impregnation agent once a year to keep the top hygienic.

A cutting board should always be used to protect the worktop. Minor damage can be repaired, for example scratches can be removed with a specially designed scouring pad. If the top has a large dent, however, a professional will be able to repair it in situ. Repairs will be invisible in most cases and will not result in loss of quality.

Plus points
- ⊕ wide selection of colours, designs and models
- ⊕ hard, durable
- ⊕ low maintenance, hygienic
- ⊕ easy to repair
- ⊕ more resistant to scratches than natural stone
- ⊕ moisture-resistant
- ⊕ heat-resistant for pans that are not extremely hot

Minus points
- ⊖ less natural than pure natural stone
- ⊖ no uniform colours
- ⊖ sometimes expensive

1 & 2. The colour of composite stone is never absolutely even. The material is available in polished and matt finishes. 3. The sink can, of course, be made from the same material as the worktop.

1. Composite stone is made of stone granulate that is compressed with resin to make a solid whole. 2. The material resists heat, scratches and acids very well. 3. As shown here, composite stone is also ideal for the splash wall.

CONCRETE
Worktops

Concrete is increasingly being used as a material for work-tops. It is already common in professional kitchens, often as an alternative to granite or composite stone, and is particularly suitable for kitchens with a modern, contemporary design. The concrete used for kitchen worktops weighs less than traditional concrete. Concrete worktops are composed of a special mixture of cement and sand, and have an average thickness of 8 to 10 cm (3 to 4 in). Sealants have to be added to make the worktop waterproof; this is done before the concrete is poured. Concrete worktops are generally available in the standard colours, but other colours must be ordered and are, therefore, more expensive. It should be noted that only pastel shades are obtainable.

Concrete worktops are usually cast on location. This must be done by professionals and requires a mould that can be placed in a fully horizontal and level position. Once hardened, concrete is difficult to process so if a sink is required in another material the cutaway must be specified beforehand. Stains can easily form as concrete is very porous and not resistant to acids. The best thing to do is to treat the material once it has been installed. There are several options for this: the concrete can be impregnated with a hydrophobic agent based on siloxanes so that it keeps its natural look, or it can be treated with a product based on polyurethane or epoxy, which will make it highly resistant to acids and give it a matt or glossy look depending on the type of product. If the worktop is treated with linseed oil or beeswax the result will be matt.

Concrete is heat-resistant, hard and resistant to scratches. The material is cold, but still somewhat warmer than natural stone. It is also smoother and easier to maintain than natural stone, although regular treatment with one of the finishing products is still recommended to prevent stains from forming too easily. Concrete is not particularly cheap.

Plus points
- ➕ durable
- ➕ low maintenance
- ➕ scratch-resistant
- ➕ moisture-resistant
- ➕ heat-resistant

Minus points
- ➖ must be cast on location by professionals
- ➖ difficult to process afterwards
- ➖ limited range of colours
- ➖ expensive

1. Concrete kitchen tops are either poured on the spot, or made of modules cemented together as in this case. 2. The material is ideal for creating an industrialised atmosphere. 3. This original solution shows just how heat-resistant concrete is.

1	2
3	4

1. Floor and worktop can easily be made of the same material, blending together. 2. When concrete is treated with oil it gets a deeper colour and resists stains better.

3. Concrete also gives enormous freedom of form, although slight flaws are often apparent in the finishing. 4. A nice example of a uniform whole.

SOLID WOOD
Worktops

A wooden worktop is timeless and has a natural, warm look. It is not only an excellent fit in a rustic kitchen design but also well-suited to linear, cool designs as it adds contrast. Each top is unique because of the different types of wood available and the structure of the individual tree. For example, maple can be used, which has a light colour, cherry with its warm colours, or dark tropical wood types. Beech is often used for kitchens because it is a relatively cheap wood. Usually the colour will change gradually under the influence of daylight. Whichever wood is chosen it can be easily processed in a variety of ways.

It is simple to glue separate pieces of wood together during installation or, alternatively, to work with small planks that are pressed together and glued. When building in a sink, allowance should be made for the fact that wood expands and shrinks as a result of temperature and humidity changes. Because wood absorbs moisture, kitchen worktops are treated with an oil-containing product and require regular maintenance afterwards. The type of wood determines the best method for this and the products that should be used. Teak, for example, is relatively soft and requires less upkeep as it contains a lot of natural oil. In most other cases, monthly treatment of the worktop is needed to prevent drying out. It is also possible to protect the worktop with a layer of varnish or lacquer rather than oil, but this is not recommended as scratches in the lacquer can allow moisture to penetrate the wood and damage it.

Stains can be removed with a moist cloth. Water should be mopped up immediately as it will leave rings if it ends up underneath an object and is no longer able to evaporate. Usually the rings can be removed with a hot, moist cloth, but if the rings have already permeated the wood the worktop will have to be sanded lightly and re-treated. It is important to clean the worktop thoroughly at all times. The wood should never be cut on directly as any notches and nicks in the worktop could cause bacterial contamination. A cutting board should be used instead. Wood is also not heat-resistant. If the worktop is damaged a professional should be called to repair it. If moisture has accumulated underneath the lacquer layer, the worktop should be returned to the manufacturer.

The price of a wooden worktop depends on the type of wood used.

Plus points	Minus points
➕ warm	➖ high maintenance
➕ natural	➖ not hygienic
➕ a range of price categories	➖ not heat-resistant
➕ wide selection of types of wood and colours	➖ not colour-fast
	➖ scratches easily
	➖ can be affected by moisture

1. All sorts of beautiful finishes are possible with wood. 2. Wood does demand quite a bit of maintenance. 3. Varnished wood stains less easily.

1. Teak is a tropical wood that withstands moisture well. 2. A wooden worktop suits any interior style.

LAMINATE
Worktops

Many people choose a laminate worktop because it is an easy material to install and maintain. Laminate is based on HDF sheeting, which is made of fine wood fibres that have been compressed to a high density and glued to make them watertight. The more the fibres are compressed, the better the quality. A pattern layer (a photo print) is placed on top and a transparent melamine layer over that. Laminate with a hard surface should be used for worktops. Laminate is available in various colours and designs, and there are matt and gloss finishes.

A laminate worktop is easy to install. If a sink or hob needs to be built into it the contours can be sawn at a specialist shop. Alternatively, a fine-toothed saw can be used as this prevents pieces flaking off the top layer and avoids a rough sawn line, which would make it easier for water to permeate. Screws should be used to attach the laminate on top of the wooden structure underneath, working on the underside of the worktop. The worktop can also be glued, but that will make it difficult to replace later on. It is important to seal all the joints using a silicone sealant, particularly around sinks, hobs and wall edges.

Laminate is not very durable; high-quality laminate lasts about ten years. It is not heat-resistant either, so hot pots and pans should not be placed directly on the worktop. Although water cannot penetrate the top layer, the laminate core is not moisture-resistant so it is important to purchase a worktop with rounded edges as the upper layer runs over the edges at the sides reducing the risk of moisture getting in. A laminate worktop should never be cut on directly as scratches or nicks will damage the top layer and may let moisture permeate. If this happens, the underlying wood will swell up, for which there is only one solution – to replace the worktop. This is also why it is not a good idea to use abrasives. Repairing the worktop if it gets damaged is not possible either and the only option is replacement. Laminate is not resistant to scouring powders and must be cleaned with soap and water. On the other hand, this material is stain-resistant.

Laminate is not as expensive as real wood.

Plus points
⊕ wide range of colours and patterns
⊕ easy to install
⊕ cheap
⊕ resistant to stains

Minus points
⊖ not heat-resistant
⊖ scratches easily
⊖ only the top layer is moisture-resistant
⊖ not durable
⊖ cannot be repaired

1. The cut edges of the laminate are often finished with a laminate strip or with aluminium. 2. Laminate and heat don't always mix well so care must be taken. 3. Laminate is very low maintenance.

1. Laminate is available in all sorts of colours and finishes. 2. This laminate worktop looks very like real wood.

SYNTHETIC STONE (CORIAN®)
Worktops

Corian® is actually a plastic composed principally of natural minerals, a pure acrylic polymer and pigments. A worktop made of this stone-like plastic can be fully customised to suit any taste. A very wide selection of colours is available, and there is a choice between plain colours and speckled or granular patterns. Another advantage of Corian® is that it is easy to combine the plastic with other materials. For example, sometimes a strip of natural stone is cemented onto the edges to stop water running off. Wood or aluminium can also be used as finishing. Corian® can be bent at high temperatures too, enabling rounded shapes to be created.

Installation is simple. The worktop is manufactured to given specifications and then screwed onto a wooden frame on location. Joints are finished with a silicone sealant to stop moisture permeating; once this finishing has been applied, the seams will no longer be visible. It is possible to use this composite material not just for the worktop but for the sink and drainage area as well. If desired, it can also be used to cover the wall behind. If the sink is to be made in the same plastic, a mould is created first and the material is then cast in it, thus avoiding seams.

People often choose synthetic stone because of its versatility, user-friendliness and strength. It is more solid than laminate and also heat-resistant. However, with a Corian® sink, it is recommended to let the cold water tap run when pouring off boiling water from vegetables in order to limit the change in temperature. Corian® is easy to maintain because it is not porous and the joints are filled in, so the worktop can be kept perfectly hygienic. The material is also waterproof. Consequently, liquid stains cannot harm it, although lemon juice, kiwi juice, tomato juice and red wine could leave marks, particularly if the worktop has a light colour. Rounded corners can be scrubbed easily, but dirt is more likely to get stuck in square corners. A worktop made of this plastic is resistant to sunlight and can also be cut on. Scratches can be easily removed by scouring and, if the worktop does get damaged, it is relatively straightforward for a professional to repair it.

Corian® is more expensive than stone and laminate.

Plus points
- ✚ low maintenance
- ✚ wide range of colours and finishes
- ✚ hygienic
- ✚ usually stain-resistant
- ✚ moisture-resistant
- ✚ not affected by acids
- ✚ scratch-resistant

Minus points
- ➖ more expensive than stone or laminate

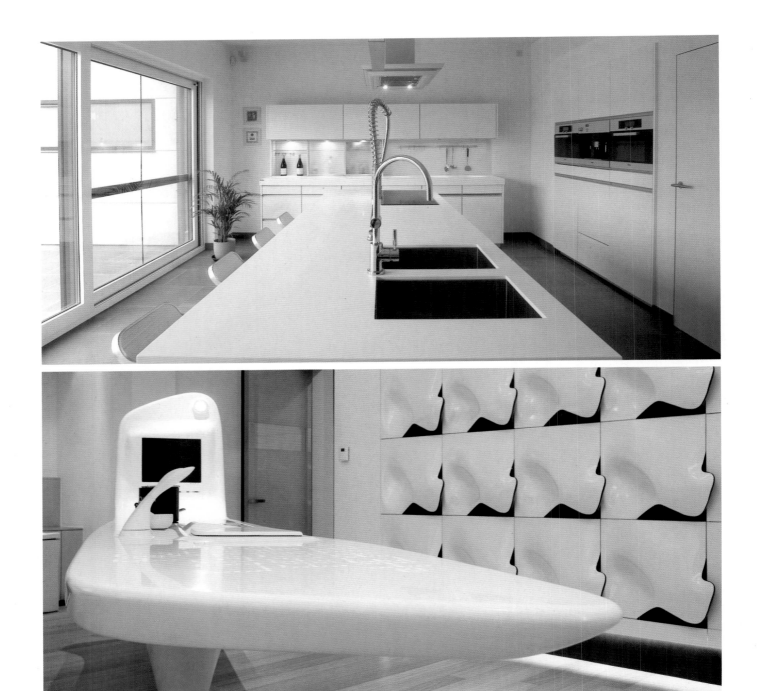

1 | 1. Corian® has an unbelievable range of benefits. 2. The material makes any conceivable shape possible.

2

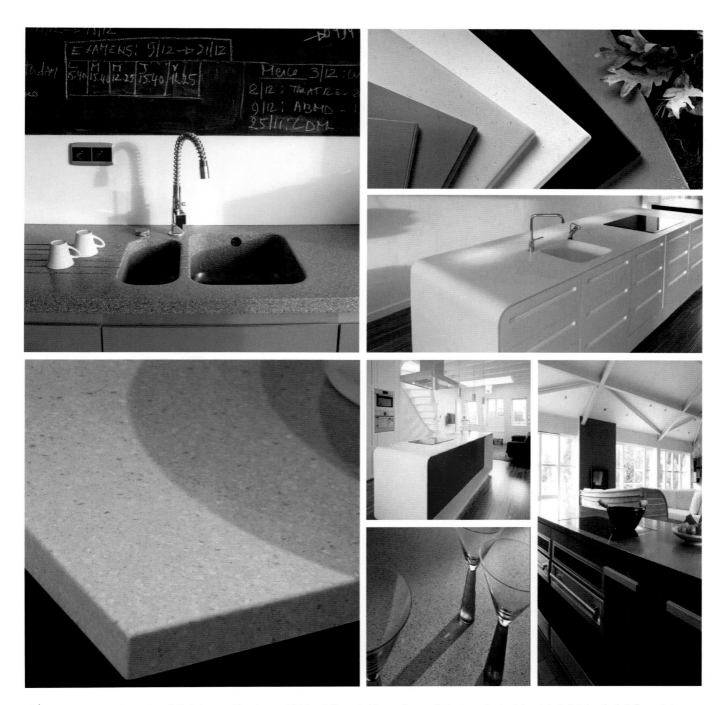

1. Synthetic stone is available in innumerable colours and finishes. 2. The material even allows particular types of natural stone to be imitated perfectly. 3. These photos show the versatility of synthetic stone in the kitchen.

STAINLESS STEEL
Worktops

Stainless steel is now a standard choice for worktops. It has been used in professional kitchens for a long time and has become increasingly common in domestic kitchens over the past few decades. Its cost has also come down. Stainless steel is made by alloying various metals, such as chrome and nickel, into the iron. If desired, it can be combined with warmer materials, such as wood, or with intense colours.

Installation involves separate pieces of stainless steel being welded seamlessly into one single piece. The thin plate is then shaped into a specific design and placed over a wooden construction. A stainless steel sink can be welded into the worktop. The surface can then be finished in various ways to get different results. If it is polished, the material will shine, while scouring will give the material a matt look and pearl-blasting leaves a silky sheen.

The material is durable but may get dented if heavy objects fall on it. The worktop can be glued onto a wooden sheet to give it sufficient solidity and prevent it from sagging. Another disadvantage of stainless steel is that it scratches surprisingly easily and a cutting board should, therefore, always be used. In the course of time, any scratches will create their own feel and blend into each other, producing a natural patina. Although the worktop may look a bit different then, its quality will not be affected. Minor scratches will be less conspicuous if stainless steel with a relief surface structure, such as corrugation or stippling, is used.

Stainless steel is heat-resistant, hard-wearing and hygienic. It requires little maintenance; it is fully waterproof and does not absorb water, oil, fat or acids. Even so, the worktop must be dried properly as dried water splashes will remain visible as stains. It is also sometimes difficult to remove persistent fingerprints. All that is needed to clean the worktop is soap and water. To remove limescale, the worktop should be cleaned with vinegar as anti-scaling maintenance products can affect the steel and should not be used. Stainless steel is a cold material.

Plus points
- ➕ moisture-resistant
- ➕ heat-resistant
- ➕ acid-resistant
- ➕ low maintenance
- ➕ hard-wearing
- ➕ hygienic

Minus points
- ➖ scratches easily
- ➖ not impact-resistant
- ➖ fingerprints are easily visible
- ➖ cold

1 | 3
2

1. Stainless steel can be finished in a variety of ways. 2. Sinks can be welded on seamlessly. 3. Although it was previously primarily a material used for professional kitchens, people are becoming increasingly aware of its benefits in their homes.

1 | 2 | 3

1. Stainless steel is extremely heat-resistant and hygienic. 2. This material is also often used for splash walls. 3. Stainless steel has a cold feel and a rather industrial appearance.

LAMINATE
Cupboard doors

Laminate is cheaper than real wood and using it helps keep down the price of a kitchen. The material for the cupboard doors (a term used here to also cover other kitchen unit fronts) can take up quite a slice of the budget. Laminate is based on HDF sheeting, which is made of fine wood fibres that have been compressed to a high density and glued to make them watertight. The more the fibres are compressed, the better the quality. A pattern layer (a photo print) is placed on top and a transparent melamine layer over that. Laminate sheets meet the highest quality requirements. For worktops laminate with a hard surface should be used, although this matters rather less for cupboards. Laminate comes in a large number of colours and patterns and can have a matt or glossy finish, so it can be used in all types of kitchens.

Laminate is often chosen because it is good value for money. It can also stand up to intensive use; cupboard doors are opened and closed many times a day and must, therefore, be able to take a few knocks. Other important advantages are that laminate does not scratch and is resistant to heat, water and steam.

Hygiene is very important in a kitchen. Fortunately, cleaning laminate is simple as it has dirt-repellent properties. Marks can be wiped off easily with water, soap and a soft cloth. It is better not to use scouring pads or abrasives as scratches will soon become visible, particularly on matt or glossy designs.

An even cheaper option than laminate is MDF (medium density fibreboard) cupboard panelling with plastic foil. The foil is glued onto the MDF under high pressure at a temperature of 120°C (250°F) and takes the shape of the front. Because of its flexibility, the foil can take on any shape and is available in lots of colours, including glossy finishes. A disadvantage is that the foil can crack or come loose under the influence of extreme heat. Even slight damage may be enough to let moisture penetrate the MDF board.

Plus points
- ⊕ does not scratch easily
- ⊕ moisture-resistant
- ⊕ resistant to stains
- ⊕ heat-resistant
- ⊕ wide range of colours, designs and models
- ⊕ low maintenance
- ⊕ good value for money

Minus points
- ⊖ not real wood

1. Photographed images can be added to laminate as a top layer, either in black or as a wood grain. 2. Laminate is sometimes indistinguishable from wood veneer.

1. Laminate cupboard fronts can also have a gloss finish. 2. Prints can be made to run across several cupboard fronts.

WOOD
Cupboard doors

Wooden cupboard finishing may be made of solid wood or a veneer. Various types of wood can be used, such as pear, cherry, mahogany and maple, or beech for kitchens with a youthful ambience.

Solid wooden kitchen cupboards consist entirely of one particular type of wood. Veneered materials are made from chipboard or MDF board with a thin layer of wood attached to it. MDF sheeting is moderately dense; chipboard is preferable. The quality of veneer can vary enormously depending on the type of wood chosen. The standard thickness of veneer is 0.6 mm ($1/_{40}$ in). A new trend is thick-sliced veneer. These thicker layers can be processed more easily, for example by sand blasting or brushing them to make the surface rougher, or by processing them to make them look like solid wood. New production techniques are also being introduced. For instance, composite veneer is made by gluing layers of dyed wood and pressing them into a solid block.

Wood has a natural pattern so that each board is a little different; this is particularly the case with solid wood. Those who prefer a rectilinear pattern should choose quarter-sawn wood in which the tree trunk is first cut into four parts and then sliced perpendicularly to the tree rings. The patterning of veneer wood is more uniform than solid wood because the veneer sheets are much thinner. Veneer wood is delivered to the processor book-matched, which means all the veneer wood from a specific tree is kept together. The book is opened to be processed into a veneer sheet, thus ensuring that the grain lines in the pattern are properly aligned. Composite veneer, on the other hand, may show a huge range of structures and colours.

Solid wood has a price tag that reflects its quality and robustness. However, this is no guarantee that the quality will be better than veneer because high-quality veneers are also available. Wood is a sensitive material and any flaws or defects will be clearly visible.

Wood is neither scratch-resistant nor heat-resistant. However, according to experts, wood is no more of a fire hazard than other materials; although wood is flammable, the way it burns is slow and predictable. Wood absorbs moisture and dirt, and kitchen doors are particularly vulnerable to these problems. Therefore, if wood is chosen as the material for cupboard doors it must be treated with a protective layer that resists grease and acids. It is important to check that the wood selected has been treated in this way. If so, the cupboard doors may be washed with standard cleaning products.

Plus points
- ✚ natural look
- ✚ warm
- ✚ authentic
- ✚ good value for money

Minus points
- ➖ flaws and defects in the material are visible
- ➖ wood needs a protective coating
- ➖ must be processed by professionals
- ➖ scratches easily
- ➖ not heat-resistant

1. Wood has a very solid look. 2. Natural oak boards give a rough effect. 3. This kitchen shows real craftsmanship.

1. It is clear here that the fronts are made of solid wood. 2. The three photos show different types of finishing: oiled, painted and patinated. 3. Wood is a sturdy material that exudes class.

RECYCLED WOOD
Cupboard doors

Tradition and authenticity are key aspects for kitchens with a rustic look. These kitchens have beautiful wooden beams, old-fashioned farmhouse tables, antique handles and so on, all of which gives them a venerable appearance. The cupboards in these kitchens are sometimes finished using time-worn, recycled materials – materials with a history.

The reuse of such products also benefits the environment. The recycling usually takes the form of old wood being used to make kitchen cupboards. These old materials come from castles, farm houses, convents, historic homes and similar places. They are very suitable for rustic kitchens, but can also be used to make kitchens with a more industrial appearance look less clinical.

Recycled wood is cleaned and treated first so that it is ready for use again and meets modern quality standards. In some cases it is also restored, which may increase the cost considerably.

Wood absorbs moisture and dirt, and kitchen doors are particularly vulnerable to these problems. Consequently, if wood is chosen as the material for cupboard doors, it must be treated first with a protective layer that is resistant to grease and acids. It is important to check that the wood selected has been treated in this way. If so, the cupboard doors may be washed with standard cleaning products. Wood is neither scratch-resistant nor heat-resistant.

According to experts, wood is no more of a fire hazard than other materials; although wood is flammable, the way it burns is slow and predictable.

Plus points
- ✚ environmentally friendly
- ✚ authentic

Minus points
- ➖ expensive
- ➖ wood needs a protective coating
- ➖ scratches easily
- ➖ not heat-resistant

1. Keeping to the same shades of colour creates a harmonious whole. 2. The recycled wood gives both these kitchens a lived-in feel.

1
—
2 | 3

1. This darker-coloured wood is good for a kitchen with a rustic style. 2. A playful and unique kitchen fits in very well in a modern home. 3. The use of recycled wood shows ecological awareness.

SINKS
Standard and designer-made

A sink gets used a great deal. There are a number of factors that need to be taken into account when choosing the material for the sink. Hygiene is important as the sink is also used when cooking, for example to rinse vegetables. This means that the sink must be easy to clean. Account should also be taken of the interior and the style of the kitchen. The material chosen needs to fit in with that style or, alternatively, the sink can be used to create a striking individual accent. For example, it is quite possible to incorporate a stainless steel sink in a rustic kitchen where large amounts of solid wood have been used.

Stainless steel sinks are the commonest choice, not least because of the favourable pricing. Moreover, they are undoubtedly high-quality sinks: stainless steel is strong and heat-resistant. It is important to dry the sink properly, however, as dried water splashes will remain visible and leave stains. One disadvantage is that stainless steel scratches relatively easily and can also make a lot of noise, for example when cutlery is placed in the sink for washing up.

Another option is to choose a sink of the same material as the worktop, such as natural stone (various specific characteristics are given in 'Kitchen worktops', pages 243 to 281). Even a ceramic sink with a protective glazed layer is possible. Ceramics are resistant to heat and scratching, but the glazed layer may be damaged by sharp objects. A plastic sink may show limescale over the course of time, so regular thorough cleaning is recommended. Copper sinks are rather special as they have an idiosyncratic look all of their own.

Sinks can be installed by placing them on the worktop or by fixing them to the underside of the worktop. When installing the sink, consideration needs to be given to where the openings for the plughole and taps should be made. Some worktops have integrated sinks: this is an option for plastic, concrete, stainless steel, glass and composite stone. Worktops and sinks are then made as a single piece, which means there are no seams and consequently no risk of moisture permeating. Another important decision besides the choice of material is the size of the sink. The best option, if there is enough room, is to have two sinks. There are also designs with one large sink and one small sink. The depth of the sink also needs to be considered; it usually varies between 18 and 30 cm (7 to 12 in). A deep sink is not advisable for tall people because they would have to bend over too much.

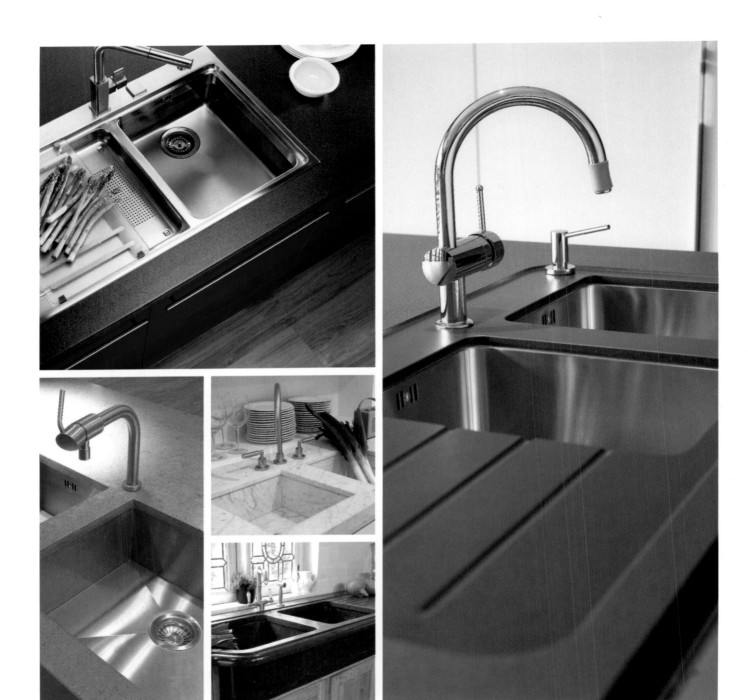

1. This flush-fitted stainless steel sink fits in perfectly with the worktop. 2. Three sinks made of different materials. 3. This is an example of a sink fitted underneath.

1. A composite stone sink can be fitted seamlessly into the worktop. 2. A sink with rounded corners is easier to keep clean than one with sharp corners. 3. The depth of the sink determines how easy it is to use.

TAPS
From classic to austere

Taps in the kitchen are used for many different things: washing up, rinsing, washing hands, making coffee and so forth.

On average, the taps get turned on and off ninety times a day, using about sixteen litres (3 ½ gallons) of water. Therefore, the key consideration for taps is that they should be functional, although their design can also add to the kitchen's look. A standard model, a design with very clean lines, a baroque style, or anything in between can be chosen.

A single-lever mixer tap, also known as a one-lever tap or one-lever mixer, is operated with one hand. The temperature is controlled by moving the handle to the left or right so that it mixes cold and hot water. The temperature and the flow can thus be controlled in a single movement. This is quicker and uses less water than a double-lever mixer tap, the traditional type with separate handles or knobs for hot and cold water.

The tap is often fixed to the sink unit, but if fitted on the wall this will create more room around the unit. The spout of a kitchen tap is higher than for other taps to allow buckets or deep pans to be filled. The spout can often be swivelled if there are two sinks so that either sink can be filled with water. Even more practical is an extendable hose that can be used to rinse the entire sink unit. The pressure can be controlled to give a powerful, targeted water jet or a more dispersed, softer jet. A bottle brush or pan brush can be attached to some models. Even more technical options are becoming available. There are taps with a flow limiter or tap aerator, which can save on water by up to 40%. A flow limiter restricts the amount of water coming out of the tap, while an aerator adds air to the water stream. There are taps that produce soda-water and boiling water, taps with a safety device to prevent burning, thermostatic taps and many other options.

Most taps are made of brass with a protective nickel layer and a final finish on top of that. Usually this is gloss chrome, but matt chrome, gilded, silver, bronze or copper designs, or even coloured plastic coatings, are all available. The more expensive brands are made entirely of stainless steel; they can easily last fifteen to twenty years and are scratch-resistant.

It is also useful to find out about the inside of the tap as well. High quality requirements should be applied to kitchen taps given how much they are used. More money often has to be paid for well-made taps.

Limescale can be avoided by regular cleaning, and dedicated products are obtainable for persistent areas. Kitchen paper or a cloth can also be soaked in vinegar and allowed to permeate the limescale. The inside of the tap can be descaled too by soaking its parts in vinegar, but first check the supplier's instructions.

1 | 3
2

1. Some taps make a statement: this one is an eye-catcher in its own right. 2. This tap design may be unexciting, but it is pretty much timeless. 3. Integrated spray heads can combine form and function.

1	2
3	4

1. Old two-handle taps are not out of place in a traditional style kitchen. 2. This single-lever tap has an unusual handle. 3. Taps can equally well be placed on the wall.

4. Three examples of different models.

BATHROOMS

FURNITURE
Washbasin units, cupboards and mirrors

The bathroom, along with the kitchen, is one of the most heavily used rooms in a home. Bathrooms come in an enormous range of prices, which largely reflect the choice of materials and the layout. Since a bathroom is not replaced very often, the best option is to choose timeless, durable materials. There is a wide range available: plastic, stone, wood, metal, etc. It is important to remember, however, that bathroom furniture must be able to resist high humidity. Chipboard and MDF are the most common materials used. Chipboard is made of glued wood fibres covered with a laminate or melamine layer as finishing. MDF has a higher density and is, therefore, better quality. Its surface is smooth and the material is more resistant to moisture.

A bathroom is an intimate room in which a person should feel comfortable, and its look and ambience are, therefore, important. Bathroom design is gaining in significance and various designers are working on creating matching collections of furniture and accessories. If a romantic, old-fashioned bathroom is desired a wooden washbasin could be used, or perhaps an authentic Art Deco cupboard might be found (but make sure it is lacquered or treated against moisture). A more contemporary look will be created if metal and clean lines are used. The cool appearance of stainless steel can be broken by choosing a warm background material, such as natural stone.

Hygiene in the bathroom is very important and bathrooms must be cleaned regularly. Ease of maintenance should be taken into account when choosing the materials. A bathroom with lots of corners and edges is harder to clean than one with fluid lines. Washbasins, mirrors and storage space are indispensable bathroom furniture and can be laid out in various ways.

A single piece of furniture that integrates the basin, mirror and cupboards could be chosen. Such a piece often has both top and bottom cupboards. This approach frees up space, making it the best solution for smaller bathrooms. Standard sets are available, but custom-built bathroom furniture can be ordered or, alternatively, separate items purchased. The hinges should always be checked when buying a piece (or pieces) of bathroom furniture: metal hinges are better than hinges that are partially or entirely made of plastic.

Consideration needs to be given to the best type of washbasin to install and whether one or two basins is preferable. The washbasin can be integrated into the furniture, which creates an attractive, orderly look, but can also be installed on a table. These built-on washbasins are more expensive than the built-in models, but fitting them is cheaper.

Rather than using a table designed for the bathroom, an ordinary table or wooden unit can be used. A very personal style can be created if unusual materials are selected.

If storage space is needed underneath the washbasin, an open space or a cupboard can be chosen. This piece of furniture can stand either on the floor or be suspended on the wall. It is important to take into account that it is also designed to hide the drain, although nowadays there are drainage systems that look good enough to be kept in view.

The minimum width of a washbasin is usually 60 cm (24 in), but if there is enough room a larger size might be considered. The washbasin height is important and is generally 80 to 90 cm (a little under 3 ft), measured from the floor. The height of the user also plays a significant role.

Many items need to be within easy reach in a bathroom. Thought should be given to these to ensure there is enough storage space. Daily grooming products, towels and accessories are essential, but space may also be required for a razor and hairdryer as well. Bathrooms used to have a single large cupboard, but in recent years the trend has been to have a number of smaller cupboards. This modular system is often

1. Using just two colours retains the clean lines. 2. Four different ways of tidying towels away neatly. 3. A stylish wooden cabinet acts as a washbasin unit.

1. Stylish furnishings are still possible in smaller bathrooms. 2. A unit with two washbasins does not have to take up a great deal of room. 3. The finishing and the details determine the style. 4. Simple cupboard doors create a functional and timeless interior.

FURNITURE (CONTINUED)
Washbasin units, cupboards and mirrors

very flexible and multifunctional, and the cupboards some-times have wheels which makes them even easier to use. Extra storage space can be provided by attractive reed or metal baskets and wooden boxes, which give the bathroom a special look. This type of built-on furniture is available in all kinds of colours, styles and dimensions. The components are very flex-ible and can easily be placed in another room.

Mirrors are indispensable in a bathroom. A small mirror used to be sufficient, but these days the tendency is to install larger mirrors. These have the additional advantage of making the room look bigger. Mirrors can be hung on the wall in the trad-itional fashion or, alternatively, cupboard doors can be fitted with mirror glass. Care must be taken to hide the sharp corners. Proper mirror lighting is crucial. Bathroom spotlights are often handy as they can be directed in whichever way suits. Side lighting or indirect lighting are best as they create the most favourable viewing conditions.

1	2
3	4

1. *In this example, the entire wall consists of cupboards.* 2. *Even a shallow cupboard provides useful storage space.* 3. *Mirror lighting should be placed down the sides to avoid casting unflattering shadows on the face.* 4. *The niches by the chimney breast have been used neatly here to fit two separate sinks.*

1	2
3	4

1. *A mirror along the whole wall makes the bathroom appear larger. 2. Indirect lighting below and above the mirror gives a friendly ambience. 3. Wall-to-wall furnishing creates lots of room for the people using it. 4. A bathroom with a lot of daylight is very pleasant, but care should be taken to provide enough privacy.*

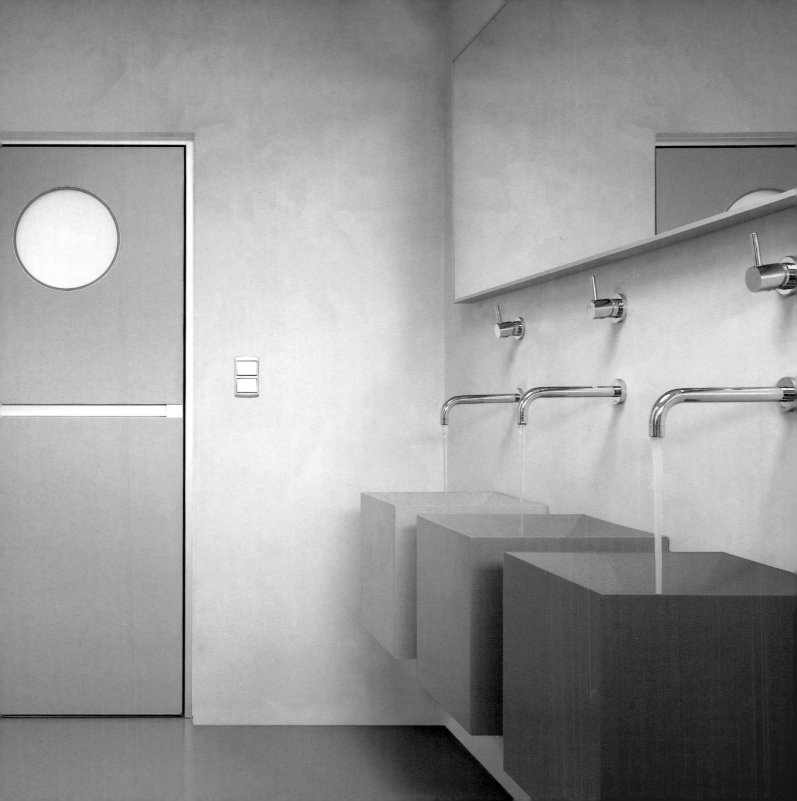

WASHBASINS
Shapes, materials and use

In the past, the washbasin was used for daily personal washing; nowadays it is mainly used for a quick freshen-up, brushing teeth or washing hands. So the washbasin's purpose has changed and the design has responded to this.

Washbasins can be round, oval, rectangular or square, and also come in different sizes. Deep basins are no longer really required as large amounts of water are not needed any more. There are currently elegant, rather flat designs on the market with depths varying from 5 to 18 cm (2 to 7 in). The standard width is 40 cm (15 ½ in), but any width can be chosen.

The first priority when selecting a basin should be convenience. Shallow basins splash easily and it is sometimes difficult to keep basins clean if they have straight or sharp corners. There also needs to be sufficient space between the wall and the basin, particularly if it is mounted on a wooden stand or cupboard, so that the back can be cleaned as well. Double washbasins are also obtainable, but are becoming less popular because they take up more space. Washbasins are not always integrated into a unit; they may be installed in a different place, for instance against the wall or on a column.

Washbasins sunk into a unit are very handy for cleaning. The washbasin and unit are made from the same material – a plastic for example – and are seamless, which makes them easy to clean. There are a number of different designs available.

Washbasins can be made of various materials. Ceramics with a very hard, smooth glazed layer are frequently used. This material is very hygienic because bacteria cannot accumulate in any small irregularities. Another material for basins is sheet steel, which weighs less and is used for less sturdy walls. The steel is covered with an enamel layer that is just as hard, smooth and dense, and as hygienic, therefore, as the glaze of quality ceramics.

Kaldewei enamel is a fairly new product on the market. This material is largely self-cleaning because water droplets do not attach to the enamel and so dirt and limescale are transported to the drainage system. The basin can simply be cleaned with a moist cloth. If wood is used, it needs to be given a thorough protective layer against stains and moisture. Water drops must be wiped off straight away. Wood durability should preferably be Class 1 (very durable). Class 2 (durable) and 3 (moderately durable) could also be used. Suitable wood types are: afrormosia (1-2); afzelia (1); azobé (1-2); bangkirai (2); bilinga or opepe (1); chestnut (2); ipé (1); itauba (1); jatoba (2); makore (1); merbau (1); moabi (1); teak (1); tola (1) and western red cedar (2).

Plastic, natural stone and composite or synthetic stone are suitable washbasin materials. Designers are also experimenting more and more with stainless steel and glass; both of these fit well in a relatively minimalist interior. On the other hand, frequent cleaning is recommended for them; soap and water is sufficient for this, while systematically mopping up water droplets will save a lot of work. One of the latest trends is to use multiple colours of natural stone, which creates an authentic, warm and stylish look, but proper support is required as natural stone is heavy. The pros and cons of the various materials can be found in the information about kitchen worktops on pages 243 – 281.

1. The eight photos on the left show just what a wide range of materials and shapes washbasins can be obtained in. 2. Unique items can sometimes be picked up at antique shops.

1. Shallow washbasins are attractive, but water does splash around more. 2. A porcelain washbasin in a modern style. 3. These photos show clearly that there must be enough distance between water sources and switches or plugs.

BATHS
Free-standing or built-in

A whirlpool, jacuzzi or sauna don't need to be installed to make a bathroom a great room to relax in; much can be achieved by choosing the right colours and materials, and through the positioning of the furniture. The bathtub plays an important role in this process.

The modern bathtub is no longer simply used for a weekly wash. It has become the focal point in the bathroom, a place to relax and unwind. Manufacturers are responding to this trend and bathtubs are now on the market that are not only very comfortable but also beautiful items of design.

The trend now is not to have a built-in bathtub but a free-standing bath in a corner, by a wall or in the middle of the bathroom. Much depends on the available space and the design of the bath. Such free-standing bathtubs are available in various styles.

Old-fashioned is hip again, such as claw-foot bathtubs. There are also baths with sides that are higher at the head end, or streamlined bathtubs with a very modern design. Oval bathtubs look good when placed free-standing in the middle of the room, as this creates a powerful visual effect. A free-standing bathtub often has steps as otherwise it can be very difficult to climb over the tub's edge. High-quality, more expensive materials are increasingly used for free-standing baths as they are such a conspicuous object in the room.

The advantages of a built-in bath are that cheaper materials can be chosen and they require less space. But even a built-in bathtub does not necessarily have to be placed up against a wall. It could be encased in the middle of the bathroom, which creates an unusual effect. The bath can be integrated into the interior by bringing the cladding up to the edges of the bathtub making it a single unit.

A luxurious option is partial integration of the bathtub into the floor so that a much smaller step is needed to get into the bath.

Baths with an overflow system are also available: water that flows over the edge of the tub is collected and recirculated into the bath water. Designers have taken up this idea, using objects like pebbles and wood to create decorative effects in the overflow area.

A standard bathtub is 150 to 180 cm long (5 to 6 ft) and 70 to 80 cm wide (27 to 31 in), which gives a choice of sizes. People who like to lie stretched out in the bath and submerge themselves can choose a longer model, though more space will, of course, be needed for it and water consumption may increase. Moreover, a larger hot water tank and boiler might be required, which may increase the energy bill.

A combination bath is ideal for smaller bathrooms as either a bath or a shower can be taken. There are baths on sale that are designed to allow showering in comfort, for example with steeper sides and often somewhat wider at the foot end.

Comfort and luxury are increasingly part of our everyday lives. Bathtub designs are becoming better adapted to our body shape, with the part for the feet slightly lower than the part that is sat in. There is also extra support for the back to prevent slipping and even bathtubs with headrests. The many bath accessories on sale these days only make bathing even more pleasurable. One example is the racks that can be placed across the bath so soaps, fragrances and wellness products are all within easy reach.

The materials most commonly used for baths are enamelled steel and acrylic plastic. However, enamelled bathtubs are becoming less popular as they have poor insulating properties, which means the water cools down quickly. This is not the case with acrylic baths. Acrylic also feels less cold to the touch, and has the additional advantage of being less slippery than steel and, therefore, safer. If there is any damage to the surface of an acrylic bath no colour difference will be visible as the acrylic

1 | 3
2

1. A free-standing retro bath is suddenly very modern again. 2. Here, the bath dominates the bathroom and there is a wonderful view of the garden. 3. Bathtubs were made of copper in the past, which meant they lost their heat more quickly.

1. In this bath, the water can overflow into catchment basins under the stones. 2. A book stand and pillow for the neck make the bathing experience even more comfortable.

3. A wooden bathtub is certainly nice and warm, but it does demand a lot of maintenance.

BATHS (CONTINUED)
Free-standing or built-in

material is coloured right through. However, scratches do leave traces so abrasive sponges or cleaning materials must not be used for cleaning. Damage to enamelled bathtubs is often highly visible as a piece of the enamel is likely to chip off. Damaged areas can be touched up using enamel paint, but the join will still remain visible. On the other hand, enamelled steel is very tough and will not scratch. One highly exclusive option, and also a very expensive one, is a bath carved from a single piece of natural stone – marble, bluestone or granite. Virtually the same effect can be achieved with a bath made of composite stone, a mixture of ground natural stone and plastic (see page 259 for more information about composite stone). Baths can also be found made from the plastic Corian®, and these are available in a wide range of colours (see page 275 for more information about this material).

A particularly original choice is a wooden bath. Since time immemorial, wood has been used in Scandinavian countries for open-air baths after a visit to the sauna. Wood creates a special atmosphere and a feeling of warmth. It also keeps the heat in, but must obviously be treated to make it properly watertight.

1. The floor covering can be extended up the sides of the bath. 2. Ceramic tiles are the most obvious finishing for the edge of the bath. 3. When placed in the middle of the room, the bath itself becomes the bathroom's eye-catcher. 4. A cheap bathtub looks more luxurious if it is built in neatly.

1	2
3	4

1. A limited range of colours produces a harmonious whole. 2. An original way of building the bath in, following its own curves. 3. A shiny finish adds to the feeling of luxury.
4. The bath can also be finished using natural stone.

SHOWERS
Materials and trends

Taking a shower in the morning has become a daily ritual for many people. Showers are obtainable in many different types and sizes.

The classic shower is a shower cubicle in which the water is collected in a shallow tray about 15 cm (6 in) deep. The most commonly used materials for a shower tray are enamelled steel and acrylic plastic. Steel is a poor thermal insulator and loses heat more quickly, whereas acrylic insulates better and feels warmer. It is also less slippery than steel and is, therefore, safer. If there is any damage to the surface of acrylic plastic no colour difference will be visible as the acrylic material is coloured right through. On the other hand, scratches do leave traces, which is why abrasive sponges or cleaning materials must not be used. Damage to enamelled steel shower trays is often highly visible, as a piece of the enamel is likely to have chipped off. Although damaged areas can be touched up using enamel paint, the join will still remain visible. However, unlike acrylic plastic, enamelled steel is very tough and will not scratch.

The walls of a classic shower unit are usually mortared and tiled, with one side consisting of a shower curtain or a door made of Plexiglas, safety glass or a translucent plastic. Glass walls are being used more and more so that the shower can be fully integrated into the room. In all cases the walls must be waterproof. Prices depend on the material chosen.

There are shower trays in various shapes and sizes; 80 x 80 cm (31 ½ x 31 ½ in) is standard, but there are also models suitable for wider or smaller spaces. Nowadays there are even shower trays without proper raised edges, which are rather similar to walk-in showers. These combine the advantage of a shower tray – low-maintenance acrylic plastic and easy installation – with the aesthetic appeal of a walk-in shower.

Modern interior design increasingly uses walk-in showers with a bathroom floor that continues into the shower. There is no visible shower tray anymore, although there is a kind of hidden tray underneath the shower surface. These used to be made of lead, but this is being superseded by plastic because the cement of the floor affects the lead after a while. Another alternative is to use a special foil. The surface above this hidden shower tray can be finished with tiles, integrated pebbles, wood and sometimes even polished concrete – there is a wide choice. However, it is important to select a material that is water-resistant and not too slithery; polished concrete, for example, is rather slippery. Walk-in showers placed at the same height as the floor have drainage systems that are positioned slightly lower. If a walk-in shower is wanted, this must be taken into account when designing the bathroom. If renovating an existing bathroom, this problem can be resolved by using a small step and placing the entire shower about 8 cm (3 in) higher.

A mortared tiled wall or matt or translucent glass is usually used with the walk-in shower to prevent water splashing everywhere. Spiral mortared walls that suggest a wave action can also be used. Obviously, the shower walls should be waterproof. The decision to have a walk-in shower fits in with the concept of the bathroom as a place to unwind. There is no shower curtain or door. Walk-in showers usually take up more space than standard showers: at least 90 x 90 cm (3 x 3 ft) for the showering area. A properly positioned walk-in shower makes it almost impossible for water to leak onto the bathroom floor. The walk-in – the passage to the shower – must be designed in such a way that there is enough room to hang a towel or a bath robe to ensure maximum enjoyment.

As well as the classic shower trays and walk-in showers, there are complete shower cubicles with the shower tray and the walls forming a single unit. These can easily be installed; all that is required is to connect up the water supply to the shower,

1 & 2. A bench or seat in the shower is often handy for children or more elderly people.

1. Acrylic shower trays are warmer to the touch than enamelled ones. 2. Safety glass must always be used in showers. It is available in all sorts of colours and finishes.

SHOWERS (CONTINUED)
Materials and trends

and the electricity if necessary. Creative, modern and luxurious designs with all kinds of technical gadgets are available: shower cabins with colour and lighting effects, with a steam function, with side sprayers, or even with a built-in radio.

The taps in a shower are also very important. A thermostatic tap adds to the comfort because it can guarantee a constant temperature when showering, and is also safe and economical. Many shower heads allow the water jet to be adjusted, whereby the smaller the holes, the more powerful the jet. Rain showers have large to very large shower heads, which give the sensation of pouring rain and are very calming. A standard technical system (pipes, drainage, ventilation, heating, etc.) is sufficient for many rain shower models, but the existing system should be checked to make sure that it meets the technical specifications of the rain shower selected. It is useful to install a small hand shower as well when installing a permanent rain shower as this makes washing away soap residues easier. Side sprayers, which spray from all directions, have a relaxing effect, but do increase water and energy consumption. Conversely, if a water-saving shower is chosen, this will consume considerably less water. This is because the shower head has integrated higher resistance, which reduces the flow of water and increases the release of air. The difference is hardly noticeable as the water jet is just as powerful, but less water is used. A further environmentally-friendly step is to install a shower that recuperates, purifies and pumps back the water.

Shower maintenance requires extra attention. The best thing to do is to rub everything dry immediately after showering as this will prevent the accumulation of scale and dirt over the course of time. This is often not really feasible because everything has to be done quickly in the morning. If there is any residue, the best way to remove it is by using an acidic product like vinegar, specifically intended for cleaning. Some products can, however, be aggressive to aluminium and rinsing with clean water quickly afterwards is recommended. Hard water contains a lot of limescale, which can block the shower-head holes, but there are self-cleaning shower heads that keep the holes free.

1

2 | 3

1. The mosaic part of this simple shower continues in the walls of the bath. 2. A harmonious transition from the floor covering to the walk-in shower. 3. A rounded walk-in shower is a unique way of protecting the room.

1. The drain of the walk-in shower should always be kept properly clean. 2. A red mosaic plus wood pattern give this bathroom a warm ambience.

TOILETS
Materials and trends

Most newly-built homes have at least two toilets. A toilet can be integrated in the bathroom or installed in a separate room. To ensure privacy when putting a toilet in the bathroom, make sure it cannot be seen immediately when entering the room. Some interior architects resolve this in a creative way: they hide the toilet bowl by building it into a concrete casing.

The toilet bowl can either stand on the floor or be suspended from the wall. Suspended toilets are often more expensive, but look better and are easy to maintain because they can be cleaned underneath. In classic models the flushing cistern is placed on top of the toilet bowl. There are also models with the flushing cistern integrated into the wall, and this is always the case with suspended toilets. All that is visible is a flush push button on the wall. An advantage of this system is that the sound of the flushing cistern is dampened.

The flushing cistern is usually made of plastic or sanitary porcelain. The toilet bowl is almost always made of sanitary porcelain, although designer models may also be available with stainless steel bowls.

A number of novel features are available for toilets. Some models have bidets for personal hygiene and hot air to ensure quicker drying. Others have soft-close seats that cannot fall down quickly onto the toilet bowl – a safe alternative for small children. There are toilets with an extraction system in the toilet bowl itself, which transports all the odours to the discharge pipe. The environment is also taken into account. Water consumption can be reduced by using a double system for large and small flushes or by using rainwater for flushing. Other environmentally-friendly techniques increase the pressure of the water jet, as a result of which less water is needed. There are stop buttons that interrupt flushing and, nowadays, there are even composting toilets on the market. These do not flush everything away but instead turn the contents of the bowl into compost. The composting toilet literally has a double bottom: one compartment for collecting the faeces, the other for composting. There are also toilets with a grinder system so that everything can be ground up and flushed through a small discharge pipe.

Original toilet seats are available in any colour and in a very wide range of patterns, including photo collages. A really striking option is a toilet seat with a translucent plastic coating and LED lighting. Toilet seats with a plastic foam layer are comfortable to sit on.

Urinals are becoming increasingly popular. They take up very little space and the flushing system does not consume much water. They often have a cover to avoid odours. Even urinals for women have appeared on the market recently.

It is important to make sure the toilet room has a ventilation system and attention is paid to maintenance comfort. For example, check that the attachment points can be cleaned properly. It may be handy to fit a small washbasin in the toilet area; one with just a cold water tap will usually be sufficient.

1. These seven photos are examples of various contemporary models. 2. A wall-mounted toilet bowl is easier to clean around.

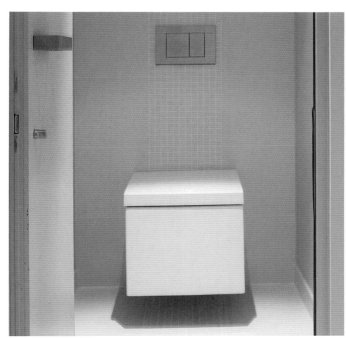

1 | 3
2 |

1. Here is an example of a square model. 2. A smaller toilet space can be delineated within a larger room. 3. Old-fashioned charm can still be obtained.

TAPS
From classic to austere

Taps need to be considered carefully because they are indispensable and used numerous times a day. The type of tap required depends on use. In a bath the tap should have a large flow in order to fill the bath quickly, but a more gentle stream of water is fine for a washbasin. This is the reason why washbasin taps have a smaller flow than bath taps.

Water is precious and should be used economically. In most cases a tap will allow the flow to be adjusted as required. Considerably less water will be consumed if a water-saving shower is installed, where the shower head has a higher resistance. This reduces the water flow and increases the release of air, but the difference is hardly noticeable as the water jet is just as strong. Showers that recuperate, purify and pump up the water can also be installed.

There are environmentally-friendly taps for the washbasin and bath as well. Using a flow limiter – a kind of filter placed on the tap – can ensure that less water flows out of the tap. The disadvantage is that the flow is always low, even on those occasions when a lot of water is needed. An intermediate solution is to use a tap with two modes: an economy mode which consumes less and a comfort mode which has a greater flow rate. It is also important to watch the temperature. There is no need to use hot water if turning the tap on and off in a series of short bursts, for example if rinsing something off. There are systems that only provide hot water when the comfort mode is switched to. Another alternative is electronic taps, which have a detection system that only lets the water flow while hands are under the tap.

Most taps are mixer taps: these are single-lever taps that allow control of the flow and the hot and cold water at the same time. Double-lever taps have separate hot and cold water handles or knobs; finding the right temperature with these can often take a while, which may mean unnecessary water consumption.

This could add up to a considerable amount over the year. Thermostatic taps are handy in the bathroom, and almost indispensable if there are children. These taps allow the temperature to be set; the rotary knob has a temperature indicator, which makes it easy to set the tap to a certain temperature. Thermostatic taps also often have a child safety lock; the knob gives a click at a certain temperature, after which a safety button has to be pushed to get hotter water. This type of tap is particularly good for showers, but less suitable for washbasins. A centralised thermostat is a means of ensuring that the water from all the taps is at the same temperature. The hot and cold water supplies are continually adjusted to give a constant water temperature, and if hot or cold water is drawn from a tap elsewhere in the house, other taps will automatically adjust. Such taps are very safe, as there is no risk of a sudden rise in temperature.

The quality of a tap depends mainly on its inside parts, as this is where the hot and cold water is mixed and the tap turned on and off. It is, therefore, important to take this into consideration. Technology has made it possible to develop high-quality, durable taps. They often cost a bit more, but on the other hand offer durability and problem-free water systems. Taps used to have washers – a rubber-based sealing system – but nowadays increasingly have ceramic discs, which may have been reinforced with a diamond layer or carbon layer. These discs start to rotate when the tap lever is moved, allowing control of the flow and temperature. The advantage of these taps is that they are user-friendly and durable, and do not leak easily. Ball valve taps have a spherical stainless steel bearing, which is as durable as a ceramic disc.

Taps are available in various designs and styles, and there are often 'designer' models. A period effect can be created with large chrome, copper or gold-coloured taps, which exude a

1. Five photos of designer taps... but beauty doesn't come cheap. 2. Wall-mounted taps are much easier for cleaning.

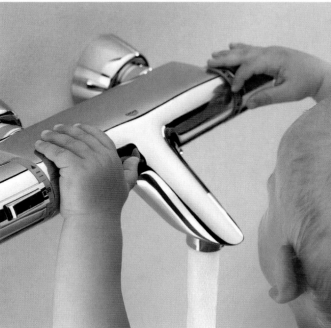

1	2
3	4

1. A wide water flow has a relaxing effect. 2. A flow limiter helps keep water consumption in check. 3. Thermostatic taps do not get too hot on the outside, so they are safe and good for children to use. 4. A single-lever tap allows both hot and cold water to be adjusted at the same time.

TAPS (CONTINUED)
From classic to austere

nostalgic mood. There is also a wide selection of handles and knobs available. A contemporary look can be created using soft, undulating lines, while other taps give a more dynamic and austere impression.

Ease of use and ergonomics also deserve attention. Taps should fit nicely in a hand and suit the requirements of daily routines. For example, there are taps with a connection for an electric toothbrush.

Taps usually do not require much maintenance. Dried water will leave stains, but these can be easily removed with water or soap. Abrasives and aggressive products should not be used because they can damage the chrome.

It is important to check beforehand that the taps match the bath or washbasin. This is not just for aesthetic reasons but also because taps can be installed in various ways. There are built-in taps and built-on taps. In built-in taps the hot and cold water is mixed in the wall and a lever or knob fitted to the wall. No holes are then needed in the washbasin or bath. If the washbasin already has holes for the taps, building them into the wall is not an option and a built-on tap must be used. With built-on taps, hot and cold water come out of the wall at separate points. The taps can be fitted onto the wall or on the edge of the washbasin or bath. Both built-in and built-on taps are available in beautiful designs. Whatever type is selected, make sure that the water jet hits the inside of the basin or bath obliquely to reduce the noise.

1. A large-diameter shower head gives a pleasantly wide water spray. 2. Shower and bath can share the same space.

1. *Sprays to the sides feel good.* 2. *For a bathroom renovation, a wall-mounted tap is the most affordable solution.* 3. *Showers use much less water than they used to.*

WELLNESS
The room to relax in at home

There has been increasing interest over the past few years in everything related to wellness. People need rest and relaxation after a hectic working day and, instead of visiting a professional wellness centre to spoil themselves, an increasing number are using their own bathrooms for this purpose. There are various options for creating a wellness space at home.

Bubble baths release air bubbles into the water, providing a relaxing effect and a light massage. The more sophisticated systems allow the intensity to be adjusted, with gently flowing bubbles giving a refreshing feel. The bubbles can be blown into the water through the bottom or the side walls. Side sprayers add to the massaging effect, especially if more air is added. There are also baths that create a rapid rotational motion in the water. Jets coming up from the bottom have a mainly relaxing feel.

Jacuzzis or whirlpools provide water massage through a flow of water and air. They have a local effect, massaging the back or the feet, for example. A relatively new feature is the haze curtain. This system is built in underneath the bath and creates a vibrating motion in a liquid, which in turn causes a thin fog to hang like a haze above the water surface. It gives a greater feeling of wellness and relaxation, as if bathing in a fairy-tale atmosphere.

The temperature of the water in a bubble bath or jacuzzi needs to be about 38°C (100°F). This can be played with: the hotter the water, the more relaxing; the colder, the more refreshing. Those who like such things can add delicate oils with various aromas to the water. It should be noted that spending too long in a bubble bath can actually make a person feel tired; half an hour will give the optimum result. Bubble baths and whirlpools are often equipped with an automatic rinsing system to ensure hygiene, but these do have to be disinfected. Pipes, heads and pump must not accumulate bacteria and should, therefore, be cleaned thoroughly.

When purchasing a bath, be sure it is well insulated so that it consumes less energy in keeping the temperature at the required level. Poorly insulated baths need much more energy to maintain the target temperature, which will result in a higher energy bill.

If there is insufficient room for a bath, a special shower is a good alternative. Hydro-massage is a system in which a small number of water jets are built into the wall to spray water onto the body. There are various types: cold water jets, a warm rain shower and so on. Some models recuperate the water, which makes these systems economical to use. Saving water also means lower energy bills, because less heating is required.

A steam shower, which creates a sauna-like effect, is fun too. Steam showers are enclosed cabins, with one-person and two-person variants available. The temperature of a steam shower is approx. 45°C (113°F) and it has a high humidity level, which together produce steam. Inhaling the hot air will cause blood to circulate faster and perspiration, which will purify the skin's pores.

Steam is also healthy because it has a beneficial outcome on colds and impure skin. However, a physician should be consulted for those with a heart condition because a steam shower activates the vascular system. There are models with programmable atmospheric effects, such as lighting, music and fragrances, although these elements can, of course, be created separately.

1 | 2 / 3

1. The right lighting is important for helping to unwind. 2. A lovely view improves the sense of well-being and relaxation. 3. A jacuzzi is the ultimate way of relaxing.

1. The flow of water in the whirlpool can be adjusted to suit. 2. Jets of water can be very relaxing. 3. This bath can be covered and then lain on.

WELLNESS (CONTINUED)
The room to relax in at home

The air in a sauna (for which a separate room is required) is much hotter than in a steam shower, with temperatures often rising to as much as 80°C (176°F). Air humidity may vary, which affects heat perception: the more humid, the higher the temperature seems to be. A sauna promotes sweating and improves blood circulation. The traditional sauna is brought up to the correct temperature with an electric heating element, while an infrared sauna uses lights that provide direct radiant heat.

When designing a bathroom, do not forget some basic requirements for the flooring, walls and lighting. A cluttered bathroom often detracts from the effect of a soothing bath. Colours also affect mood: blue is calming, green is refreshing and activating, and yellow stimulates.

1. *Three examples of wellness features.* 2. *A sauna in a house is definitely a luxury.*

1. Tanning without the sun. 2. Several people can use a sauna at once. 3. A hearth and sauna in a large room – the ultimate relaxation.

HEATING
A face-lift

Warm bathrooms feel comfortable and are also less likely to suffer from condensation; water from humid air condenses much faster in a cold room, causing damp walls, fogged mirrors, and so forth. The classic heating elements in a bathroom are radiators, which are available in various designs. There are the traditional radiators, which are often placed under a window, but radiators with a horizontal tube structure are also common. These are designed in such a way that towels can be hung on them, hence their other name of 'towel dryers'. They are placed close to the wall so that there is hardly any loss of space. The bathroom determines the size of radiator required, although new techniques allow smaller radiators to be made that provide as much heat as larger models. These are often made of sheet steel instead of cast iron, and heat up more quickly. They also look good but are somewhat more expensive. Designer radiators are increasingly used as a decorative element in the bathroom.

Underfloor heating gives a feeling of comfort, and avoids having to step onto a cold floor after a hot shower or bath. It also frees up all of the walls in the room for other uses. A disadvantage of this kind of heating is that it takes quite a long time to warm up. It produces radiant heat, which ensures that the air humidity is kept at the right level. Underfloor heating hardly requires any maintenance and prevents dust from circulating. However, both the installation and the system itself are expensive. The floor must be properly insulated and the best floor covering is, therefore, tiles or some types of stone because they retain heat well.

Mirror heating prevents condensation on the mirror after a shower or bath and stops the mirror fogging up, but is not usually enough to heat the entire bathroom.

It is very important to consider the safety of any heating devices in a bathroom. People are still dying each year from carbon monoxide poisoning through faulty equipment. Carbon monoxide, an odourless, colourless and poisonous gas, is produced by incomplete combustion of carbon-containing fuels combined with insufficient ventilation. The supply of oxygen and the discharge of flue gases must work perfectly to prevent this happening and it is vital, therefore, to ensure proper ventilation and to have the devices inspected by a professional every year. Check also that the pilot flame of the boiler is blue and not orange.

1 | 2
3 | 4

1. A round vertical radiator distributes the heat well. 2. A radiator in front of the window is the most effective arrangement for avoiding cold spots in the room. 3. Add a unique element to the bathroom: a radiator with a wood-look finish. 4. The heating capacity of a slatted radiator is generally less than that of a full panel.

1. This ornamental radiator is a real eye-catcher in the room. 2. Various designs for integrated floor heating elements. 3. These five photos show various possibilities for bathroom heating.

LIGHTING

LIGHTING IN GENERAL
Types of lighting

Artificial lighting is not merely useful – it also affects emotions. It can be used to create different moods that improve the sense of well-being. There are various forms of lighting available and designers have done full justice to the range of options, with beautifully designed lighting systems as a result. It is important to think lighting through carefully and never to purchase lights randomly; lighting has a major impact on an interior and there are many alternatives. Having the right light is very important and should come first, followed by the design.

It is always vital to make sure there is enough light and to take this into account at an early stage. All too often, the lighting is only added once everything else is in place and it then turns out to be too bright, too clinical or to cast annoying shadows. A useful approach is to draw up a lighting plan showing the number of light sources and the kind of light desired. Various factors play a role in such a lighting plan, like the intensity, warmth and colour of the light. Specialists can also be consulted who will help combine the different aspects. For example, some interior designers specialise in lighting advice, drawing up a lighting plan together with the architectural plan.

The required light intensity depends on a number of factors. For example, the angle of natural incidental light is crucial and maximum use of it should be made. The interior is also important: if this is relatively dark, stronger light sources may be needed. Awareness of how the light is reflected is crucial – a light-coloured wall will give a different result to a dark one. It is important as well to take account of what a light source is being used for, and where people might want to read, sit cosily or have to work. Spaces and work areas can be lit in such a way that allows everything to be done without being blinded, or a pleasant environment can be created that exudes a feeling of calm. Dimmer switches are very handy for adjusting light levels to suit the circumstances. The light fittings themselves can affect the light intensity too: some lampshades are dark and let only a little light through, and some lamps have filters that reduce or distort the light intensity.

Another important aspect to take into account is the colour of the light, which can be influenced in various ways. There are coloured bulbs on the market, with some types of light bulbs providing warm light, for instance if the glass is terracotta-coloured. The interior of the lampshade also affects the light colour; if it is gold-coloured, the light will be warm. Dimmer switches used in combination with halogen lighting create a warmer colour when the light source is dimmed.

There are four types of lighting that can be included in a lighting plan. The basic lighting is the most important; it should provide a nice, even distribution of the light without causing too many irritating shadows. Direct light sources are most commonly used for this, but indirect lighting is also possible if it is well thought out and applied carefully.

The second type is functional lighting. This provides support for various activities such as desk work, cooking etc. at specific locations. It is important to avoid sharp contrasts with the surrounding area.

The third type is effect lighting, which is particularly suitable for creating a specific atmosphere. Spotlights are used to pick out an artwork, for example, or make a reading corner more comfortable. Effect lighting can also be used to enlarge a space visually, making a room appear wider or emphasising architectural elements to give the interior and the materials used a certain distinction. The light should not be too bright and if used in spaces where a computer is used it must not cause any reflections.

The fourth type is orientation lighting. This is a weak light illuminating a certain route but not strong enough for small details. This type of light can be left on during the night and can help a

1

2

1. This office uses other light sources in addition to daylight. 2. The right lighting can emphasise the architecture.

1. Bookcase lighting is both functional and attractive. 2. White light is cooler and suits designs with simple lines.

LIGHTING IN GENERAL (CONTINUED)
Types of lighting

person find his or her way easily in the dark, for instance if going to the bathroom or using the stairs. LED (Light Emitting Diode) lighting is well suited for this.

When drawing up a lighting plan, a decision must be made on how to position the light sources. While in the past people worked on the assumption of a single central light source, nowadays there are far more options. Movable lighting, which can be positioned to suit requirements (see page 411), is very handy, although there should be plenty of sockets placed around the room to avoid laying long cables across living spaces. There is also built-in lighting, which can be embedded in walls, cupboards, floors, ceilings and so forth (see pages 391 and 402). Another option is built-on lighting that is attached to the wall (see page 391) or the ceiling as in hanging ceiling fittings (see page 399). Designers have always shown considerable interest in fittings, which can add a great deal to the lights themselves. Almost anything is possible. There are small, delicate designs, as well as expressive, sculptural ones. One trend is minimalism with its stripped-down lines in a tight interplay, but the more traditional circular and oval fittings remain popular. Fittings also play a role in the way the light is dispersed, with indirect light providing a softer ambience than direct light. If uplighters are used account needs to be taken of the distance to the ceiling, as the larger the zone being lit, the greater the amount of reflection. The effect of uplighters will largely be lost if the ceiling is dark because it then absorbs all the light.

There are technical choices to be made too. There are three main types of light. The first type are standard incandescent light bulbs (see page 371), although these are rapidly disappearing, and halogen bulbs (see page 375). Both of these have a filament in a glass casing. The second type consists of fluorescent tubes (see page 379) and energy-saving bulbs (see page 383), also known as CFLs (Compact Fluorescent Lights). The final type

consists of LED lighting, another type of light source that does not have a filament (see page 387). A LED has two semi-conductors that light up when electric current is passed between them. In the past they were mainly used for displays or as indicator lights for electronic devices, but nowadays they are often found as a light source in an interior. Their great advantage is that their light intensity can be adjusted.

The following table gives an idea of the power consumption of the various light types.

Light bulb (incandescent)	40 – 100	watt
Energy-saving bulb	15 – 20	watt
Halogen spotlight	10 – 15	watt
LED light	0.2 – 5	watt
Fluorescent tube	8 – 58	watt

However, the relative power consumption does not always correspond to the amount of light or the light intensity (expressed in lumens) provided for that power. A certain type of light of a given capacity may generate a different light intensity to another type with the same power rating. Obviously, lights with low consumption and high intensity are more energy-friendly than those with high consumption and low intensity. A 58-watt fluorescent tube provides four times as much light as a 100-watt light bulb. Fluorescent tubes, particularly the later T5 types, are therefore more energy-efficient than incandescent bulbs. The output of a 100-watt Osram light bulb is 1340 lumen, whereas a 20-watt Dulux EL Longlife energy-saving light gives 1230 lumen. A normal 50-watt halogen light provides 910 lumen, whereas a 50-watt IRC halogen light provides 1250 lumen. At the time of writing, the light output of LED lights is approx. one and a half times greater than the yield of halogen lights with the same rating, but this is increasing fast and the

1. Spotlights on a stair help keep it safe. 2. Accent lighting draws attention to specific elements. 3. This light has the same clean lines as the interior.

1. Sculptural light fittings give the interior a personal touch. 2. This wall fitting points the light both upwards and downwards. 3. Light as an objet d'art.

LIGHTING IN GENERAL (CONTINUED)
Types of lighting

theoretical limit is about three times as high as a T5 tube.

Occasionally it may be necessary to replace existing lights and fittings in order to consume less electricity and live in a more energy-efficient home, a process known as 'relighting' or 'lighting' renovation. The investment will often pay off within five years. Lights must have an energy label, whereby Class A is the most energy efficient and used for energy-saving lights, while Class G is the least efficient and used for incandescent bulbs (which is why they are increasingly being phased out in Europe). Light bulbs should, therefore, be replaced by energy-saving bulbs, particularly in locations where lights are on for much of the time.

Following a few practical tips can allow a lot of energy to be saved, even without replacing lights. It is a cliché, but frequently forgotten nevertheless – switch off the lights on leaving the room! Electricity consumption can also sometimes be limited by using dimmer switches, but this is not true in all cases as some dimmer switches continue to consume energy in their rest position. A smart solution is to reduce standby consumption by installing an on/off switch between the socket and the dimmer switch or transformer.

Technology enables lighting to be turned on only when needed. Consumption can automatically be reduced through the use of timers, daylight sensors or motion detectors. A rather new, but increasingly widely used system, is 'domotics', which allows everything to do with lighting to be pre-programmed. There are simplified domotics systems that are set up for lighting only and can be extended for other applications at a later date.

1. A spotlight above a mirror creates shadows on the face. 2. These spotlights radiate a lot of heat as well as light. 3. Light sources at different heights create a dynamic within a room.

1. This type of lighting accentuates the structure of the brick wall. 2. Fluorescent lighting is efficient.

INCANDESCENT BULBS
Light sources

The classic light source is a glass bulb containing a tungsten filament that is heated by an electric current until incandescent. The white-hot filament provides light, but a light bulb inevitably radiates heat as well because the light is merely a side-effect of the heating. At best, no more than 10% of the energy used by the bulb is actually converted into light. The rest is radiant heat or infrared, and the efficiency is, therefore, low. The filament becomes thinner over the course of time until it breaks, which interrupts the circuit and the bulb no longer works – it has 'blown'. The average life of an incandescent light bulb is about a thousand hours. The higher the filament temperature the whiter the light, which reduces the proportion of radiant heat. More light is emitted as a result, but at the cost of reducing the lifespan of the filament. As a consequence the bulb will not last as long. The colour rendering of incandescent bulbs is perfect.

In the distant past, the glass shell contained a vacuum so the filament could not burn. These vacuum bulbs were larger and made of thicker glass. Heating caused the filament material to slowly evaporate and deposit on the inside of the glass. Over more recent decades, the bulbs have also contained an inert gas (almost always primarily argon). The pressure slows down the darkening of the glass. The glass of these gas-filled bulbs is often extremely thin because the round shape is well able to withstand the pressures due to heating.

There are various types of light bulb available. Bulbs that have clear glass provide direct light, while opaque glass is less dazzling and creates a more diffuse effect, and silver-topped bulbs can be used for indirect light. There are also coloured bulbs that can be used to create a particular ambience, and special bulbs for use in humid rooms and outdoors.

Incandescent light bulbs can be used throughout the house, but for financial and environmental reasons they are most suitable for areas that do not need to be lit up for long periods, such as a shed, cellar or toilet. The advantage is that this type of light bulb can take being switched on and off frequently. When purchasing a light bulb, it is a good idea to check its wattage, which must not exceed the maximum capacity of the fitting. A transformer is not needed to connect this type of bulb to the mains. Incandescent light bulbs are fairly cheap.

Plus points
- ✚ wide range
- ✚ fairly cheap
- ✚ good colour rendering
- ✚ can take being switched on and off frequently

Minus points
- ➖ high energy consumption
- ➖ limited life

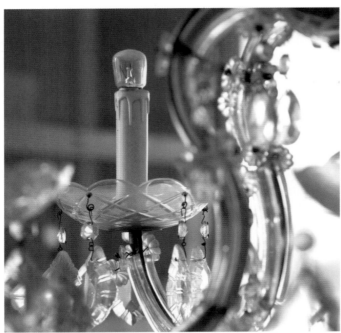

1 | 3
2 |

1. A light bulb based on a candle. 2. These bulbs are almost inconspicuous. 3. A classical chandelier can be made more subtle by putting a semi-translucent shade around it.

1 | 3
2

1. The higher the temperature of the filament, the whiter the light. 2. A number of low-wattage lights together give enough light. 3. Textiles, particularly fabric lampshades, have a warm and cosy look.

◀ Halogen lights are available with a range of beam width angles.

LIGHTING   375

HALOGEN LIGHTS
Light sources

A halogen bulb is a variant on the light bulb theme, with a filament that is heated white-hot by electricity and which then emits light. Halogen bulbs, therefore, radiate heat too, as the light is the result of heating. Unlike normal light bulbs, they also contain halogen gas that creates a chemical compound with the atoms of the filament as they evaporate. This stops the deposit of the metal, so the glass does not darken. The gas also allows the evaporated atoms to reflux back onto the filament in what is known as the 'halogen recycling process'.

Some halogen bulbs use a low voltage and others work at mains voltage. Low-voltage halogen bulbs always need a transformer, which is placed near the bulb or the distribution box. This is why these lights often have to be built into a lowered ceiling, so that the transformer and cabling can be placed out of sight. The light from low-voltage halogen bulbs is whiter and brighter than the light from a light bulb or a high-voltage halogen bulb, which is why these bulbs are often used for large areas, such as driveways and stairwells. Because they use low wattages, their electricity consumption is less than incandescent light bulbs, making them cheaper. They have a lifespan of up to five thousand hours. The latest low-voltage halogen bulbs have a coating for infrared thermal radiation that reflects the heat from the bulb back onto the filament. As a result, they emit 30% more light without using extra energy and have a longer life as well.

High-voltage halogen bulbs use the normal mains voltage and do not need a transformer. Their light is stronger than a traditional light bulb and they have a maximum lifespan of two thousand hours. There are currently various types of energy-saving halogen bulbs on the market, with a specially wound filament and additional inert gas to make sure that the heat stays inside the bulb. This means savings of 20% to 30% without losing light intensity.

The radiation angle, which can vary from ten to sixty degrees, is a relevant feature as the larger the angle the better the light will be dispersed. This is particularly important when halogen bulbs are used for general lighting. Halogen reflector bulbs have bundled light, making these bulbs ideal for effect lighting. Halogen bulbs are more expensive than incandescent light bulbs, but they last longer. However, it is important to make sure that they are properly connected as the lifespan advantages of the halogen bulb will be lost if the voltage is too high. Some types of halogen bulb have the same fitting as incandescent light bulbs.

Plus points
➕ longer life than an incandescent bulb
➕ lower energy consumption than an incandescent bulb
➕ no dark precipitation
➕ a low-voltage halogen bulb is brighter than an incandescent bulb

Minus points
➖ more expensive than standard light bulbs
➖ the light may be too bright
➖ low-voltage halogen lighting requires a transformer

1 / 3
2

1. A single halogen light can still give a lot of illumination. 2. These blocks produce very focused lighting. 3. Built-in and independent lights allow plenty of variation.

1. A modern lighting element in a stately town house provides an interesting contrast. 2. Five examples of halogen lights with their own specific designs.

FLUORESCENT TUBES
Light sources

Everyone is familiar with the fluorescent tube, a low-pressure gas discharge tube containing inert gas and mercury vapour. Such fluorescent tubes cannot be connected up to the mains but need a ballast, a kind of coil that limits the current and helps heat the two electrodes. The current creates an electric discharge in the gas, causing the mercury vapour to emit invisible ultraviolet light in the tube. The inside of this tube is coated with a fluorescent powder that then converts the UV light into visible light.

Traditional fluorescent tubes have a lifespan of ten thousand hours and use less energy than light bulbs, making them ideal as environmentally-friendly alternatives.

Fluorescent tubes require the ballast both to start up and to keep on giving light. Depending on the type of ballast, their lifespan may get up to twenty thousand hours, or even fifty thousand hours in the case of special XT tubes (Long Life tubes).

Various diameters are available, the most common types being T8 and T5, with tubes of 26 and 16 mm respectively (approx. $1^1/_8$ and $^5/_8$ in). T5 tubes were specially developed for use with electronic ballasts and must, therefore, only be connected to this type. These tubes are slightly more expensive, but the light will illuminate more quickly. The lifespan, at twenty thousand hours, is double the standard lifespan and the energy consumption drops to about a quarter in comparison with classic fittings or devices. Electronic ballasts also make sure that defective or worn-out tubes cut out safely, and the light produced is more restful.

Fluorescent tubes used to emit a cool, rather industrial light with colours that were somewhat unnatural. This was due to the composition of the powder inside the fluorescent tube. Nowadays, different powders are used and the colour representation of the tubes is far more natural. Moreover, they also last much longer these days without any loss of light intensity.

Fluorescent tubes are very well suited for locations that need light for longer periods and are, therefore, often used as functional and basic lighting, for example in workplaces or offices. But there are variants that emit a warmer light and, if used in combination with an attractive fitting and a dimmable ballast, these tubes can serve as atmospheric lighting.

Plus points
✚ long life
✚ low energy consumption
✚ good colour representation, depending on type

Minus points
➖ requires a ballast if this is not included in the fitting

1. Attractive fittings also allow fluorescent tubes to create atmospheric lighting effects. 2. Fluorescent lights can be linked together ad infinitum. 3. Warmer shades of fluorescent tubes are now available.

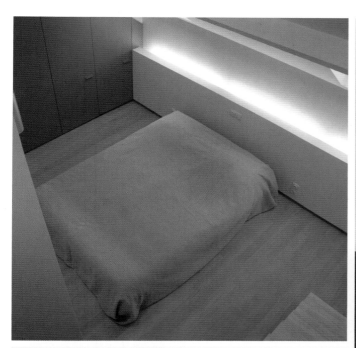

1. This kind of light can even provide soft effects in the bedroom. 2. Fittings with frosted glass produce a more subtle kind of light. 3. An example of various ways of using fluorescent lights.

ENERGY-SAVING BULBS
Light sources

Energy-saving bulbs work in the same way as fluorescent tubes. They are, in fact, small, curved versions of these tubes, hence the alternative name of CFL (Compact Fluorescent Light). The bulb contains inert gas and mercury vapour, and a built-in ballast controls the current, which also runs through two electrodes. The current creates a gas¼ discharge that makes the mercury vapour emit invisible ultraviolet light in the tube. The inside of the tube is coated with a fluorescent powder that converts the UV light into visible light.

Like fluorescent tubes, these bulbs consume very little energy. However, the shape and light colour of these bulbs are becoming increasingly like those of normal incandescent light bulbs, and they also fit most fittings. They can, therefore, be used in different ways to fluorescent tubes.

An energy-saving bulb consumes as little as one fifth of the energy of an incandescent light bulb and will last three to fifteen times longer, depending on its quality. When replacing a light bulb by an energy-saving bulb, the power rating of the light bulb should be divided by approximately five. For example, a 60-watt light bulb emits as much light as an 11- or 12-watt energy-saving bulb. When purchasing new fittings, it may be worthwhile checking that they are also suitable for energy-saving bulbs. Energy-saving bulbs are more expensive than incandescent light bulbs, but the investment pays off after as little as one or two years. The more expensive types are often more durable and retain their light intensity for a longer period. Cheaper types last about three thousand hours, expensive ones up to fifteen thousand hours. There are energy-saving bulbs with a chip that records the number of hours, and if these bulbs stop working before the specified lifespan has been reached, they can be exchanged for a new bulb.

Some energy-saving bulbs have normal screw fittings while others have a switch built into the foot of the fitting. There are also energy-saving bulbs with on/off switches and two or four positions, which permits some adjustment of the light intensity. Energy-saving bulbs with a bayonet fitting do not have a built-in ballast and can only be used in special fittings incorporating a ballast. Nowadays, there are energy-saving bulbs that can be dimmed using a normal light-bulb dimmer switch. There are also spotlights with energy-saving bulbs built into reflectors; these offer a choice between cool and warm light, but the colour representation is less natural than spotlights with incandescent light bulbs or halogen bulbs. A special type of energy-saving bulb exists for lights that are frequently switched on and off, which can also be used with a timer.

Plus points
⊕ low energy consumption
⊕ energy efficient: higher light output per watt of electricity consumed
⊕ longer lifespan than an incandescent light bulb

Minus points
⊖ certain types require special fittings
⊖ colour rendering of spotlights is less good

1. Any light bulb can be replaced with an energy-saving equivalent. 2. Using this type of light source produces considerable energy savings.

1. Energy-saving lamps can also create a homely ambience. 2. Some types of energy-saving lamps can be connected up to timers.

LED LIGHTING
Light sources

LED lighting is becoming increasingly popular. LED (Light Emitting Diode) technology is based on diodes made of semi-conductors. These light sources have no filaments, but instead consist of two semi-conductors that emit light when supplied with an electric current. LEDs require a DC power supply, converting the mains voltage into low-voltage direct current.

The first LED lights produced back in 1969, emitted red light but were soon followed by LEDs emitting green, amber, blue and cool white light. Nowadays, even a warm white light is possible. LED bulbs have a number of advantages compared with incandescent light bulbs and fluorescent tubes. Firstly, they use considerably less energy than incandescent light bulbs and although LED lights are still nowhere near optimum efficiency, the technology is developing extremely fast. Secondly, LEDs are very durable and pretty robust. Thus the material is much more durable than a glass bulb. Also, LEDs last a very long time so that they hardly ever need replacing, although there is a loss of light intensity over the course of time. The current generation of LEDs often only need replacing after fifty thousand hours. This makes LEDs suitable for installation in places that are hard to access. If LEDs do have to be replaced, this usually also involves replacing the fitting.

LEDs do emit heat, even though their light beam has no infrared radiation, and still have to be fixed on a cool surface so that the heat can be discharged, or else the LED light will soon break. The maximum temperature is approx. 60°C (140°F). Metal is often used to absorb and discharge the heat, so LED lights may have large casings, although the size of these should reduce as they become more efficient.

There are more and more applications for LEDs in an interior, particularly because the new designs emit warm white light. Colour rendering, however, is poorer than with incandescent light bulbs or halogen bulbs, and so far not even quite as good as energy-saving bulbs. LEDs are suitable for use as orientation lighting or for coloured atmospheric lighting. They can also be used outside, for example as garden lighting, although they do then need to be properly protected against moisture permeation.

LEDs are still rather expensive, though they may start coming down in price in response to increasing demand and new applications.

Plus points
- ⊕ very long life
- ⊕ low energy consumption
- ⊕ very durable

Minus points
- ⊖ if replaced, this usually means that the fitting has to be replaced as well
- ⊖ large casing may be required to discharge heat (as yet)
- ⊖ colour rendering less good than energy-saving bulbs and halogen bulbs (as yet)
- ⊖ expensive (as yet)

1. LEDs that illuminate the treads make staircases safer in the evening and at night. 2. LEDs are available in various colours. 3. It is also possible to use LED light sources to create special effects.

1. Older versions mostly produced cool white light. 2. LED lights can also be used outdoors. 3. LEDs last a very long time and hardly ever have to be replaced.

BUILT-IN AND INDEPENDENT LIGHTING
Fittings

Built-in lighting is lighting that is fitted in walls, cupboards, floors and ceilings; independent lighting is just attached to the surface.

If the lighting is built into the ceiling, there should always be enough space to install the fittings. If only installing small spotlights, at least 10 cm (4 in) of space is still needed. The built-in lighting for new construction or renovations must, therefore, be properly planned beforehand. Sometimes the ceiling has to be lowered. If an existing home already has a lowered ceiling, it is often undesirable to lower it further and install built-in lighting. If, however, a lot of independent fittings need to be attached to this lowered ceiling, the appearance might be too distracting as it could create a heavy, overloaded look. In such cases, using built-in fittings could still be considered by lowering the ceiling by the smallest possible distance. Although the ceiling is then even lower, visually it may create a more peaceful result than if too many items are attached to the surface. Built-in lighting is very handy for halls and stairwells as space is gained; often an advantage in what are frequently small or narrow parts of the house.

Holes have to be made to install built-in lighting. If prefabricated materials are chosen for a newly built house, the holes can be made to size by a reputable company; this is even possible for prefabricated concrete. If the built-in fittings have rims, somewhat larger holes can be cut. The fittings are then placed smoothly in the holes and the rims nicely camouflage the cutaways. If the fittings are to be sunk into the ceiling completely, the holes must be measured very accurately. A box is then placed in each cutaway and the fitting attached to this box. The surface of the ceiling can be given a smooth finish by careful plastering.

Built-in lighting can also be installed in walls. The same depth will be needed in that case too. It is important to make sure the lighting is out of reach of children. In addition, account should be taken of eye-levels and the fittings hung at a height of at least 1.75 m (5 ft 8 in). Ground-level lighting is always built-in to prevent people from tripping over it.

The locations of built-in materials should be kept fairly general rather than specific, as spaces in a house are increasingly multifunctional, and it should be possible to adjust the lighting to meet requirements. Built-in lighting becomes embedded in the house in a fixed location and this could be a disadvantage unless the structure of the house has been taken into account from the beginning, aligning the positioning of the built-in fittings with other fixed components, such as windows and doors. The fixed built-in fittings can be combined with flexible lighting elements, such as floor lamps.

The choice between built-in lighting and independent lighting has no impact on light intensity, but it does affect the incidence of the light.

Built-in lighting is ideal if light falling from above in a downward direction is desired, and it may also be suitable for lighting that does not need to be redirected or swivelled much. If a light source with a precise target is wanted, independent lighting should be chosen because it offers many more options. An intermediate solution is a built-in fitting that protrudes from the ceiling a little. This provides a greater degree of angular flexibility than with fully built-in lighting. Built-in and independent lighting can also be combined. Low background lighting plus bright spotlights creates a powerful ambience, enhancing contrasts and giving a cosy feeling, while brighter background lighting plus low-level spotlights creates a cooler look. Depending on the technical options, built-in fittings can also be used for background lighting or spotlights.

1. The built-in spotlights here highlight the walking areas. 2. The positioning of built-in lighting is fixed and unchangeable.

1. Some built-in spotlights can still be tilted and swivelled so that the light is pointed elsewhere. 2. Floor spotlights have to be built in completely so that people cannot trip over them.

BUILT-IN AND INDEPENDENT LIGHTING (CONTINUED)
Fittings

If there is a choice between built-in and independent lighting, their different visual effects should be considered. Independent fittings are meant to be seen and may, therefore, be attractive in their own right, an aspect that can be put to use in an interior. Some lamps and accessories are meant as decorative elements rather than as light sources. All kinds of styles are on sale in any size and price. A trend in fittings is to use designs from the past, but incorporating new technological applications. Modern designs often have defined contours with mainly straight lines and hardly any frills. If a fitting needs to be as inconspicuous as possible, built-in lighting in the wall or ceiling can be used. Technology is creating more and more options, and the evolution in electronics is making it possible to work with much smaller fittings.

Built-in fittings are cheaper in terms of the materials, but installation requires considerable professional knowledge and labour, which increases their cost, so they may come out as more expensive than independent lighting.

1. Some independently mounted lighting is all about the aesthetic aspects. 2. Mounted rather than built-in fittings were logical here.

1. Fittings with clean lines, creating a contrast in an older building. 2. Visually, the light here is nicely chosen. 3. Independent lighting mounted on the wall leaves it all but intact.

◀ Hanging lights are available in all sorts of shapes and colours.

LIGHTING   399

HANGING FITTINGS
Fittings

The term 'hanging fittings' has many meanings. In principle, it includes all types of lamps that are fixed to the ceiling with a wire allowing the lamp to swing – a flexible lamp. Suspended lamps can often be hung at whatever height suits, or the light directed from the mains power supply point to another location. The fittings are fixed with steel wires and a single cable ensures the supply of electricity.

Chandeliers have been around for centuries. Someone once had the idea of putting candles around a copper sphere, which reflected the light of the flames. Small glass crystals were used later on, and when electricity was introduced those crystals were hung somewhat lower to reduce the brightness of the light. The suspended lamp increasingly became an essential part of the interior. Wealthy people made them into splendid centrepieces, such as those enormous Venetian chandeliers.

Nowadays, there is a much wider selection of hanging lights. A hanging ceiling lamp is meant to stand out: it can be chosen to suit taste and to match an interior. Each style and trend has its own fittings, ranging from simple, cheap paper ceiling lamps, through to ones specially designed for an interior, which are of course more expensive. A trend in recent years has been to recreate authentic old chandeliers using modern materials. Ceiling lamps can function as a softening element in minimalist interiors and an eye-catching design should always be chosen. Hanging lamps are well suited for use in dining rooms: white table linen and silver cutlery will reflect the light, which increases the festive feel.

Ceiling fittings can be designed to take a powerful incandescent light bulb, a halogen bulb on mains power or multiple low-voltage halogen bulbs. It is now also possible to create an attractive look with modern dimmable fluorescent tubes.

Suspended fittings can be used for all types of lighting: basic lighting, functional lighting or effect lighting. Make sure that the light intensity does not dominate the entire room. The height of the lamp plays a role too and should take account of the height of the people using the room. It is not at all pleasant for a person to have a lamp with a very bright light shining right into his or her eyes when sitting at a table. A hanging lamp with a large lampshade should, therefore, be hung well above eye-level, but it is less annoying if the light from translucent shades shines into a person's eyes. If using halogen bulbs, make sure that the distance between the transformer and the bulb is not too great; in most cases the maximum is about 2 m (7 ft). The distance between the top of a worktop and the light should be about 75 cm (30 in).

1. Combinations of lights create a powerful impression. 2. These lamps have a reflective effect that adds to the space.

1.The best height is about 75 cm (30 in) above the table. 2. This hanging light was certainly designed to be seen!

GROUND-LEVEL SPOTLIGHTS
Fittings

Spotlights are often used in houses, particularly as functional lighting and effect lighting. Using ground-level spotlights has become increasingly popular over recent years as uplighters are very good at creating a warm atmosphere; an intimate, restful ambience is important and lighting plays a crucial role in achieving this.

Ground-level spotlights are always built-in, which is only natural as it stops people tripping over them. They are usually made of aluminium, which is durable and a good conductor of heat. The upper side of the spotlight is finished with virtually unbreakable safety glass. Although new standards state that glass surface temperatures must be restricted by using double glass, spotlights with a single layer of glass may still be on sale; these can become extremely hot if a normal halogen bulb is used, sometimes getting up to 140°C (280°F). Not only is this dangerous because of the possibility of burns, but it may also pose a fire hazard, for example if a piece of paper is dropped onto the light. It is, therefore, recommended that the glass should be checked when buying ground-level spotlights.

If choosing a double-glass ground-level spotlight for halogen bulbs, 12V halogen bulbs or LED bulbs that fit a halogen fitting should be selected. If a powerful beam is not really required, ground-level spotlights with energy-saving bulbs can be used.

In principle, ground-level spotlights and nothing else might be used for small spaces, but this creates a very theatrical effect. Floor-level spotlights can be used in a corridor or stairs if desired, as these are passages, and they can also be used as orientation lighting. However, in living areas ground-level spotlights need to be combined with other types of lighting. Bathrooms are increasingly been used for relaxation and floor-level lighting can help create an appropriate atmosphere. It is perfectly possible to install floor-level spotlights in bathrooms or other humid areas, but they do have to be waterproof, which means using spotlights suitable for use outside, e.g. for terraces or gardens. A disadvantage of ground-level spotlights in a bathroom is that holes in the floor have to be made, which is then no longer waterproof. It is important, therefore, to be very careful with the finishing to avoid any water permeation. Floor-level spotlights are often used in bathrooms in combination with a walk-in shower, or they can be installed in the edge of the bath, which will create a very powerful effect.

1. Some floor-level spotlights have an LED light. 2. This type of atmospheric lighting is being used increasingly in bathrooms.

1
—
2 | 3

1. Floor spotlights are 'uplighters' that direct the light upwards. 2. Floor-level spotlights in a hall are very functional. 3. Fluorescent tubes have been used as atmospheric floor lighting here.

PROFILE FITTINGS
Fittings

Profile fittings are fittings made from extruded aluminium. Individual extrusion profiles have a maximum length of 6 m (20 ft), but the pieces can also be fitted together, creating extremely long profile fittings. All kinds of attachment brackets are also available. Profiles can be made to size and can be constructed in such a way that a light module can be attached at any position across the full length.

Profile fittings can be built into walls or ceilings, although this requires rather a lot of space; to hide all the wiring needs 19 to 25 cm (8 to 10 in).

Profile fittings can also be attached as independent lighting, hung on the ceiling using tubes or steel wire. A wide range of surface profile fittings is on offer – all kinds of colours and designs are available and they can be made or lacquered to suit taste.

One of the advantages of profile fittings is that the profile can be fed at a certain point and then the wiring continued to be fed into it. The light can be taken from the mains voltage supply point to another location using a profile. Hanging profile fittings also make it possible to combine lighting pointing upwards and downwards, using the principle adopted by floor lamps. General lighting is pointed upward, while the shade points indirect light downward.

Profiles are useful in offices and large spaces, but are also suitable for modern interiors. Horizontal profiles are most common but vertical profiles are possible as well, although they usually have an extra function, such as delineating and dividing spaces.

Profiles are rather expensive. Their advantage is that it is possible to combine various types of light source – for example, a fluorescent tube and a halogen bulb can be fitted in the same structure – although this is not yet very common in practice. If combining different light sources, then, it may be useful to install separate switches and dimmer switches. Replacing the various parts is as easy as with separate bulbs.

1. This profile fitting fits perfectly with the clean lines of this interior. 2. The length of this fitting is the same as the kitchen block.

1

---

2 | 3

1. *This hanging fitting combines upward and downward light. 2. Profile fittings can be a good solution in large rooms with concrete ceilings. 3. An example of a designer fitting with clean lines.*

MOVABLE FITTINGS
Fittings

Interior lighting should be a combination of basic lighting, functional lighting and effect lighting. Free-standing lamps are the last elements to be included when drawing up a lighting plan, but should still be taken into account from the beginning. Although a movable lamp can obviously be shifted to a different location, it is useful to know where to install the switch and how the wires should be placed. Sockets can also be installed in the floor, if wished. It is certainly a good idea to make sure there are plenty of sockets as this will avoid having lengthy cabling running across the room.

There are large free-standing lamps, which are placed on the floor, and smaller models designed to be put on furniture, such as a cabinet or side table. It is also possible to obtain several lamps in the same design but different sizes, which creates a uniform look and emphasises the interior.

A movable lamp provides not only light but also an inviting atmosphere. It can be used to pick out certain elements, such as specific architectural features. Movable lamps are particularly common in living rooms, standing next to the sofa or close to the television, but they can also create a warm ambience in the bedroom. They are a standard fixture in traditional interiors, but have a place in ultra-modern designs as well, where they can be used to introduce warmth in an otherwise austere space. Built-in lighting can tend to have a cooler look, which can be softened through the use of a floor lamp. Movable lamps are crucial if a house has disagreeable dark corners.

Although primarily decorative, some movable lamps, such as reading lamps may have a useful function as well. Free-standing lamps with a separate, smaller flexible reading lamp on the same base are available. Some light designers try to avoid the need for a reading lamp by drawing up a balanced, well-thought-out lighting plan. The idea here is that general light sources should provide enough light for all kinds of activities including reading, while free-standing lamps are only used as decorative elements to create a mood.

The switches of free-standing lamps can make an annoying buzzing noise, which is usually caused by a poor combination of dimmer and lamp, or by the poor quality of the lamp. Low-voltage halogen lamps may have a dimmer switch that is not tuned to the transformer. Good dimmer switches do not buzz – a point to check when purchasing.

1. The standing lamps in this bedroom add to the pure, soft atmosphere. 2. The advantage of a lamp like this is that it can be moved around.

1. This heavy designer lamp is perfect as the main lighting in the room. 2. A movable lamp gives a homely feel in an otherwise rather austere interior.

LIVING ROOMS
Light in a room

A living room makes great demands on lighting as a lot of time is spent there and it is the scene of a wide range of activities. An inviting atmosphere and cosiness are important, but at the same time sufficient light intensity is required as this is where books and newspapers are read, television is watched, friends entertained, etc. Children may also have a play area in the corner. Moreover, the activities taking place in the living room may change over the course of time. Part of the living room is often used as a dining area, which requires a different kind of lighting again. The living room is the perfect room for expressing personal style. Finally, it is a space with daylight, which can vary depending on the weather and the time of day. Flexibility is, therefore, important and a combination of different kinds of lighting is required.

It can be quite a puzzle to work out how to combine the different functions and types of lighting. The first thing to do is to check the degree of light intensity required. Dark walls absorb light more easily and will need a higher wattage. It may be handy to use gradations: starting with good basic lighting, but then making the intensity less than what is actually required and using other light sources to compensate. One or more spotlights can be focused on art objects, while a floor lamp can give a dark corner in the sitting area an appealing look. Neutral white light can be used to highlight paintings or pictures as this will bring out their colours. Matt glass should be used for photos in glass frames to avoid reflections. A surprising effect can be achieved by combining light sources as this gives a certain initial impression when entering the room, and one that is gradually refined the more time is spent there.

Extra consideration should be given to a seating area; a movable reading lamp can be very handy here. A hanging lamp – one that cannot shine into a person's eyes – should be hung over the dining table. A lovely effect can be created by having the fitting match the shape of the table. Being able to vary the intensity of this light is important as a different type of light is more appropriate for breakfast or while reading the newspaper than for an intimate dinner with friends. Soft wall lights can add to the mellow ambience. White bulbs or coloured ones can be chosen that create a range of accents, but the different effects should complement each other nicely.

1. Using wall lighting means that the splendid ceiling here remains intact. 2. Using different light sources creates an exciting interior.

1 | 3
2

1. Symmetrical wall lighting emphasises the room's classical style. 2. The shape of the lampshades is repeated everywhere, creating uniformity in the lighting. 3. The choice of lighting is one factor that determines the desired look and feel.

◀ *This wonderful eye-catching chandelier might usually be expected in a living room, but it is not out of place in this big kitchen.*

LIGHTING   419

KITCHENS
Light in a room

Not only is the kitchen an area where food is stored and cooked, it is also increasingly a place where people eat and live as well. This trend has led to the introduction of the kitchen island, open kitchens, beautiful appliances and designer furniture. Lighting, therefore, now needs to fulfil two functions: it has to be sharp and bright to allow a person to work safely, but it also has to create an intimate ambience.

When considering kitchen lighting, it is important to take account of the natural incidental light and avoid having the light shine on the back when standing at the sink as this will mean working in shadow. But the light sources should not be blinding either. Another key consideration is to achieve an even dispersion of light rather than having certain zones well lit, while the areas next to them receive much less light. It should not be forgotten that a kitchen contains a lot of chrome and metal objects which reflect the light.

The best way to start is to plan the basic lighting as this will ensure sufficient light everywhere. Then thought should be given to the functional lighting above the worktop, above the cooking area or underneath wall cupboards. This can be supplemented by decorative lighting. If wall lighting is used, it should be installed at a sufficient distance from heat sources and water. In the past, fluorescent tubes were often used as a central light source, which used to create a rather clinical atmosphere. The modern tubes emit a softer light, which is usable but not recommended as the dominant light source. However, they are sometimes built into walls, near a sink unit or underneath a wall cupboard. When choosing ceiling lamps, the radiation angle of the light needs to be taken into consideration. Free-standing light sources are not recommended for a kitchen as they can be a major hindrance given that kitchens need to be cleaned frequently. Spotlights are sufficient for the basic lighting in small kitchens, but there needs to be proper angular dispersion of light. In contemporary kitchens rail systems with spotlights attached over kitchen islands or loose kitchen work blocks can be used. Incandescent light bulbs or energy-saving bulbs may be more appropriate in a kitchen with a traditional or rustic character.

Atmospheric lighting should be used in moderation because it is so easy to overdo it. Kitchens often contain a lot of colour anyway, for example in fruit and vegetables or in kitchen appliances and implements, and understated effect lighting can emphasise this. If the kitchen is often used for eating in, atmospheric lighting can be installed to allow the cooler main lighting to be switched off, or lighting with a dimmer switch can be used.

1. Hanging lights are logical and functional for high ceilings. 2. Light bulbs are more suitable above the island in a more rustic kitchen.

1. This profile fitting has been integrated beautifully into the kitchen. 2. The warm light of the fluorescent tubes is reflected on the white walls. 3. Spotlights provide focused light.

BATHROOMS
Light in a room

The primary lighting in a bathroom is important because high-quality light is required for personal grooming. Safety is also a key issue, as water and electricity are not a great combination – which is particularly relevant in bathrooms. The advice of an electrician is, therefore, recommended to prevent accidents, both major and minor. Basic lighting is usually built into the ceiling, which avoids the need for free-standing and hanging lamps. All light sources should be installed at a safe distance from the bath and shower, and special fittings are needed that are resistant to warm water vapour and splashes.

These restrictions do not stand in the way of creative options for functional and effect lighting as designers take them into account; also, the technical possibilities have recently improved considerably. Some fittings are entirely waterproof and can be used in the shower cubicle as well. Other fittings can be installed underwater, in a bubble bath for example, which creates a highly original aesthetic look.

Bathrooms are increasingly becoming an area for relaxation and wellness, where taking a bath goes hand in hand with soft, luxurious towels and wonderful scented soaps. Cold white light can destroy this feeling of wellness. In contrast, wall lighting pointed upward can create a soft background light that does not blind when lying in the bath, although the fittings must be in a safe position. Atmosphere can also be created by focusing light on specific bathroom elements, such as the water or glass objects, or colour effects might be used. It is worth considering dimmer switches for the basic lighting in the bathroom, or even just for the functional and effect lighting. The colour of halogen lighting will be warmer when it is dimmed, which will enable the right mood to be created to match the activity at that particular moment.

Mirror lighting is delicate lighting. If the light comes from behind this will create a flattering mirror image, but if the light is too bright it will have the reverse effect: wrinkles and other cosmetic defects will be more visible. The best option is to use soft lights on either side of the mirror, which prevents deep shadows being cast on the face. Some bathroom furniture has built-in lighting, which automatically switches on when the cupboard door is opened.

The choice of the type of light affects the style created. Incandescent light bulbs are warm and fit better with classic interiors, while halogen lights are cooler and have a more modern look. Finally, as much use of daylight as possible should be made.

1. Soft light at the sides of the mirror, as used for theatrical make-up, makes a person look his or her best. 2. Some lighting has been designed especially for rooms where water is used.

1. Soft, indirect light creates a relaxing atmosphere. 2. An example of lighting on a mirror. 3. These fluorescent tubes emphasise the length of the wall.

BEDROOMS
Light in a room

A bedroom has a number of functions and, therefore, requires a combination of several types of lighting. First and foremost, a bedroom is a room to unwind in. It is one of the most personal and intimate rooms of the house, and using adapted lighting and attractive fittings allows for a very personal look. But bedrooms are partly living spaces as well: clothes are stored and picked out there, television may be watched and books read, and there may also be a zone for personal care or working. Functional lighting is recommended if ironing and laundry are sorted in the bedroom.

Good primary lighting is particularly important. It should be neutral, which can be achieved by using a number of different light sources, although it is important to make sure that the lights can be switched on and off from in bed. It is important not to use blinding or very bright light. Centralised ceiling lighting can be annoying when in bed – eyes are naturally drawn to light sources. Wall lighting behind the bed is a better option, but make sure the lights shine upwards as this will provide proper background lighting and a feeling of warmth and security.

A lamp placed on a night stand is handy and this should be taken into account when positioning the sockets. It is important that the lamp can be switched on and off easily from in bed and in the dark. Reading lights should be installed along the centre line of the bed as this allows the lights to be pointed outwards, which is less disturbing for any bed partner. If possible, the reading lights should also be arranged so that the light intensity can be controlled: there should be enough light to see the pages but it must not shine into the eyes. Flexible lamps are the easiest to use, in particular because reading is sometimes done lying down and sometimes in a sitting position.

Wardrobes with built-in lighting are also available. Additional lights can be added to mirrors; this should be done at the sides to avoid annoying shadows. Whatever type of lighting is chosen, dimmer switches are a good option for a bedroom as they let the light intensity be adjusted to requirements.

Children's bedrooms need a modified approach. It is important to be prepared for various situations, because the older the child gets, the more light sources will be needed, for example if the bedroom later has to be used as a place to study. Special attention should be paid to safety. Unused sockets in the bedrooms of toddlers and small children should be covered, and free-standing lamps should not be used as they could get in the way when children are playing and are dangerous if they fall over. It is important to make sure that children cannot touch or unscrew the light bulbs.

1. Small reading lamps will not disturb a sleeping partner at all. 2. Being able to turn the lights on and off from in bed is convenient.

1. Symmetry creates peace and order. 2. The standing lamps match the white decor of the bedroom.

Photo Credits

2voor5 Publishing
Bieke Claessens
Tierrafino
Floor Concepts
Jan Liegeois
Bolon
B.I.C.
Limited Edition
Blackstock Leather
Forbo Flooring
Santana
Di Legno
Oog3
Interiann
ISO Arch.
Moso International BV
Par-ky
Pergo
Moma
Cotto d'Este
Kerlite
Beltrami
AID Arch.
Bart Van Wijk

Klaar Bracke
Isabelle Bijvoet
Arte
Eijfinger
Het Charmehuis
Geoffroy Van Hulle
Flamant
Gag
Pelckmans Watrin
Janssens
Tilly Cambre
Van der Voort Interiors
Arcobaleno
Dankers
Atmosphère & Bois
Abet laminati
Vectogramm
Orac
Litracon
Aksent
Frako keukens
Blum
Cousaert Van de Donckt
Quick-Step®

DuPont
Poggenpohl
Alno
Franke
Grohe
Vola
Anyway Doors
PIZE Porseleinatelier
AID Arch.
Starck X
Duravit
Niveka
Hanolux
Jaga
Delta Light
Kreon
De Scheemaerker
Feel at Home
Anthracite
Hal2
Toon Saldien
Lobby
Henny Waalwijk
Restyle XL

Every care has been taken to trace copyright holders of the images. However, if there are errors or omissions, the publisher would like to apologize and will, if informed, make corrections to any future edition.

©2011 2voor5 Publishing

Schoolstraat 9, B-2235 Houtvenne, Belgium

www.2voor5.be

info@2voor5.be

Concept and realisation: 2voor5

Design & interior layout: 2voor5

Authors: Hilde Pauwels, Barbara Bossier (Floors)

Photographers: 2voor5, Bieke Claessens, Jan Liegeois

Special thanks to: Paul Vermeer Kreon

Published by Vivays Publishing Ltd

www.vivays-publishing.com

This edition © 2011 Vivays Publishing Ltd

English translation: Mike Wilkinson

Editor: Clare Wilkinson

Typesetting: Deul & Spanjaard Boekproducties, Groningen

Cover design: Ute Conin, Cologne

Printed in China

ISBN 978-1-908126-12-2

All rights reserved.
No part of this publication may be reproduced or trans-
mitted in any form or by any means, electronic or mech-
anical, including photocopy, recording or any information
storage and retrieval system, without prior permission in
writing from the publisher.

Although the publisher has taken the utmost care in com-
piling this publication, neither the author, the editor nor
the publisher can accept any liability for damage caused
by possible errors or omissions.